IN THE LIONS DEN

IN THE LIONS DEN

The Rebirth of Great Britain in Rugby League

LES BETTINSON

THE KINGSWOOD PRESS

First published in Great Britain in 1991
by The Kingswood Press
an imprint of Methuen London
Michelin House, 81 Fulham Road, London SW3 6RB

A CIP catalogue record for this book
is available from the British Library
ISBN 0 413 64680 7

Typeset by Falcon Typographic Art Ltd,
Edinburgh & London
Printed in Great Britain by
Redwood Press Ltd, Melksham, Wiltshire

Contents

ACKNOWLEDGEMENTS

All the photographs in this book
have been reproduced by kind permission
of Andrew Varley.

1

Finding the Phoenix

Those who were at Boothferry Park, Hull, on Saturday 30 October 1982 for the first Test between Great Britain and Australia saw the destruction of the cream of British Rugby League by Frank Stanton's 'invincible' Kangaroos. The tourists won the match 40–4, scoring eight tries without conceding one, yet it was not so much the statistics as the manner of the victory that shocked the watching crowd. They could only marvel at the awesome power of the Australians and the speed, precision and silky skills of players who were to dominate international rugby for years to come. Brett Kenny, Peter Sterling, Mal Meninga, Wayne Pearce, Eric Grothe and Ray Price seemed to have come from another planet, whereas Great Britain appeared to be inferior not only in strength and speed, but also in ability and tactical awareness.

The Kangaroos went on to win the second and third Tests by similarly comfortable margins, outscoring Great Britain by nineteen tries to one and rattling up 99 points in all. In confusion and disarray, Great Britain's eight-man selection committee used thirty-two different players in the series without ever producing a plausible combination; only one player, Des Drummond, appeared in all three Tests. Overwhelmingly superior in all departments, both on and off the field, Stanton's team returned home in December unbeaten in the twenty-two matches they played in Great Britain and France.

Ray French, the BBC commentator, admitted prior to the series that despite his patriotism he feared the worst. He had visited the Australian training camp and seen the players undergoing various training routines carried out with total commitment under intense pressure, some involving repeatedly hitting tackle bags and shields with controlled ferocity. Such intensity was alien to British thinking at that time. French knew then that Great Britain would not be able to withstand such pressure and would have difficulty coping with Australia's power rugby – courage would have nothing to do with it.

The product of the intense Sydney competition was clearly superior to Great Britain's. Standards had not fallen in this country but neither had they improved; in the meantime, Australian standards had risen in a

spectacular fashion. Enlightened people in Britain had been predicting this for some time, certainly since the late 1970s. The writing had appeared on the wall in the Test series of 1978 and 1979. Although Peter Fox's ageing team brought off a famous victory in the second Test at Odsal in 1978, Australia gave notice of their impending supremacy with an emphatic 23–6 victory in the third Test at Headingley, to take the series 2–1. The gulf between the nations was underlined by the fate of Eric Ashton's British Lions in Australia in 1979. Although they won two of the three Tests in New Zealand, they were comprehensively routed in two of the Australian Tests and whitewashed in the series.

After that, Johnny Whiteley, the coach of the victorious Lions tourists of 1970, and Colin Hutton, the Great Britain manager, tried to inject some sophistication into the preparation of the national team. However, their results were still poor. A drawn series with New Zealand was followed by a deflating defeat at the hands of France in Marseilles. Rod McKenzie, senior lecturer in physical education at Carnegie College, Leeds, was recruited to assist with the conditioning of the players, and although he maintained that fitness levels had improved significantly under his instructions, he knew that he was only putting a finger in the dyke. On the eve of the arrival of the 1982 Kangaroos, Colin Hutton publicly declared that Great Britain had nothing to fear from these tourists. In private, he admitted to the Rugby Football League council that 'we are light years behind Australian standards'.

The reasons for the superiority of Australian Rugby League in the 1980s were not difficult to discover. I was able to confirm these for myself when I visited Sydney and Brisbane on a short fact-finding mission in 1986 in the company of Maurice Bamford, the then Great Britain coach. The key factors to emerge at that time were that Rugby League in Australia compared to Great Britain enjoyed a higher profile; a marketing strategy; greater media and public interest; more intense competition; better facilities; more efficient club organisation and administration; superior player recruitment and development; and modern coaching techniques.

During the 1970s leading Australian coaches, such as Jack Gibson, Frank Stanton and Terry Fearnley, visited America to study grid-iron methods of fitness training and team preparation. They quickly implemented some of those ideas in the Australian club system, placing greater emphasis on fitness and conditioning, defence and the 'big hit'. Alien terms such as game plan, yardage, tackle count, possession count, control and the kicking game became commonplace, and slowly but surely a more dedicated, efficient and tactically aware breed of player was produced. The Sydney competition became more and more intense and cut-throat, and the game boomed, attracting higher sponsorships and more TV exposure, with players able to gain greater financial rewards. By 1982 the Australian Rugby League Test player was superior in all departments to his British counterpart.

The British game during the 1970s, with a few exceptions, did not develop or progress as it should have done. Coaches still followed outdated

Opposite Des Drummond was the only Great Britain player to appear in all three Tests against the all-conquering Australians in 1982. His subsequent international career, however, was marred by injury and controversy.

training schedules dominated by laps of the field, sprints, moves and touch football. Players trained on two evenings a week and were paid winning or losing money. The 'retain and transfer' system still operated, and outstanding players could gain greater financial rewards only through being transferred and receiving an illegal financial inducement – a 'back hander'. Because all clubs operated on similar lines, the game still seemed relatively entertaining as a spectacle as British spectators had nothing to compare it with and still naïvely clung to the belief that British players were more skilful than the Australians. That myth was exploded in 1982. Even then, it was not until the introduction of outstanding Australian and New Zealand players at clubs such as Wigan, Hull, Hull KR and Leeds, after the lifting of the international transfer ban in 1983, that the British game realised the benefits that overseas players gained from training five days a week in their own time. They proved that weight training didn't slow you down, that even basic skills needed to be practised, that diet and discipline was important.

When Colin Hutton and Johnny Whiteley stood down from international duties after the 1982 Test series, I was particularly keen to fill the post of Great Britain manager as I believed that reform was necessary if the British decline was to be reversed. Although I was chairman of the Rugby League coaching committee my influence over international preparation was limited. The position of manager carried status and clout which would enable me to revise the outdated policy of international selection by committee and the outmoded methods of preparation, and would also help the grassroots work of the coaching scheme. The manager's brief was to include the 1984 Lions tour of Australia and New Zealand, and it was a position that would be ratified by the full council – or so I believed.

I had been attending the Rugby Football League's council meetings as Salford's representative since 1978 so I was pretty conversant with its complex micro-politics. In those days the council operated two major committees: the finance committee and the international rules committee, of which I was a member. This latter committee was chaired by Bill Oxley of Barrow, a former chairman of the Rugby Football League, who was a brusque, powerful personality and a formidable adversary. Although technically it was not the responsibility of the committee to appoint the Great Britain manager, nevertheless it was on the agenda. Following the heavy defeats by the Australians, and in view of the gravity of the crisis in the British game, surely great care was to be taken over such a crucial appointment?

Bill Oxley called the meeting to order, announced the business of appointing the Great Britain manager, and said, 'Hands up those who are interested.' I, along with several others, raised my hand. Bill then said, 'Right, we'll take a vote and reduce the numbers to two.' An open vote followed, and we were all invited to indicate whom we favoured. The result of this straw poll was that Dick Gemmell of Hull and myself emerged as the two main contenders. Bill asked Dick and me to leave the room.

Reg Parker of Blackpool, a former tour manager himself, intervened and suggested that we should be invited to make a statement. 'Not necessary,' said the chairman, 'everyone knows Dick and Les well enough – it would be a waste of time.'

I left the room in a state of incredulity. I could not believe that such a charade was actually happening and that I was part of it. Dick and I indulged in small talk as we waited for the vote. He told me that he had not lobbied anyone, which seemed, under the circumstances, an odd thing to say. When we returned, the chairman announced that Dick had won the vote and was duly elected Great Britain manager.

Dick Gemmell was a former international who had served on the 1979 tour as business manager. When asked on his return to present his financial report Dick said that there were still a few accounts to be settled, but he was confident that there would be a profit of £100,000. The tour in fact declared a loss of £30,000. Dick was obviously not a man for fine detail, and such inaccurate accounting hardly recommended him to be appointed tour manager. Yet appointed he was, by a shambles of a system that exemplified why the international team was in such a parlous state.

Johnny Whiteley's successor as coach was Frank Myler. Frank had been an outstanding player and captain of the victorious 1970 Lions tourists. He was also a respected club coach with Oldham, and he genuinely believed that if he chose the right players and got the defence right we were still capable of beating Australia. To this end, selection of the team was handed over to Myler and Gemmell, although the old selection committee retained powers of ratification.

Myler discarded the bulk of the generation who had failed so miserably against Australia in 1982, and threw the emphasis on youth in the build-up to the 1984 Lions tour. Ronnie Duane, Garry Schofield, Ellery Hanley, Joe Lydon, Garry Clark and Andy Goodway all joined Lee Crooks and Brian Noble in the Test team, and four successive victories over France were recorded in the early parts of 1983 and 1984. Yet Myler's concentration on defence meant that these were narrow, joyless wins, and although the continued good work of Rod McKenzie meant that fitness levels continued to rise and there was an air of freshness about a Lions squad whose average age was 24, there was still a definite question mark over the amount of ground that had been made up since 1982.

History records that Great Britain lost all six Test matches in Australia and New Zealand in the summer of 1984. Dogged by illness and injury, the Lions earned considerable plaudits in Australia for their perseverance, their courage and their willingness to learn. However, Ray French's verdict was that 'the party as a whole was simply not good enough ... and the weaknesses within the game in Britain were more than evident as the tour progressed'. He added that the physical inferiority of the British players, when faced with the bigger, stronger and fitter Australians, and their general tactical naivety, were significant factors in their defeat. By the time the Lions arrived in a wet New Zealand their shattered resistance crumbled in the face of a powerful and emerging Kiwi team.

Once again, Great Britain were back to square one, for all the spirited performances of Schofield, Hanley, Goodway, Tony Myler, Drummond and Lydon, who proved that they could compete at the highest level. Frank Myler resigned as coach and Dick Gemmell returned to Australia to take up a new life. He was censured by the council in his absence for not producing a tour report.

British Rugby League now waited to see what action would be taken by the governing body. Just as there had been no strategy for change in 1982, no coherent policy had emerged by 1984. There were plenty of people with ideas, and one or two with a clear grasp of what was needed, but the governing body had not appointed a commission of forward-thinking people to provide the necessary blueprint for action. They reverted to the tried and trusted approach, which was to appoint a new coach – even though there existed no plan of campaign, no job specification, no guidelines. Whoever was to be appointed would need to be some sort of messiah capable of working miracles.

In October 1984 the post of full-time Great Britain coach was advertised, and there was a strong field of applicants which included Peter Fox, Malcolm Reilly, Roger Millward, Maurice Bamford and Allan Agar. They were interviewed by the new nine-man management board, introduced in May 1983 as an executive body to handle the day-to-day running of the Rugby Football League. All the candidates acquitted themselves well and presented excellent ideas on the changes necessary to bring about a renaissance in the British game. In the end, Peter Fox of Bradford Northern and Maurice Bamford of Leeds emerged as the leading contenders.

In many ways they were similar in background, experience and enthusiasm. Both were confident and articulate and made first-class presentations. In terms of track record Peter Fox was well ahead, with many league and cup triumphs. He had already coached Great Britain against Australia in 1978, and had introduced many unique ideas to team preparation such as quoting lines from inspirational poetry. In the end, established players resistant to change undermined his authority and influenced club officials and council members against him. Thus, when the position of coach for the 1979 Lions tour was debated, the manager, Harry Womersley of Bradford Northern, recommended to council that Peter Fox should fill that position. This did not receive popular support, however, and Eric Ashton of St Helens won by a large majority. Peter carries the scars of that rejection to this day.

Maurice Bamford was currently enjoying much deserved success with Leeds, who were going well in the league and had won the John Player Trophy in January 1984. Maurice had coached for many years, mainly with less fashionable clubs, and at one period had assisted Peter Fox at Bradford Northern. Maurice had an outgoing personality, loved coaching and had infectious ideas about patriotism. He was popular throughout the game,

The much-travelled Maurice Bamford, whose motto might well be that which appeared above the door of the Dewsbury dressing-room. Bamford succeeded Frank Myler as Great Britain coach in the autumn of 1984.

and his enthusiasm and openness impressed the interviewing committee.

Because Peter Fox was regarded by the media as 'controversial', and because there still existed the remnants of the prejudice against him which had persisted since he was coach of Great Britain in 1978, opinion began to move away from him. When the vote was finally taken Maurice Bamford won the day by a short head. For Maurice this was the realisation of his dreams and aspirations; the management board was confident that he would tackle the job with total commitment. Ironically, his position at Leeds was filled by Peter Fox, and two years later Maurice was to return to Leeds following Peter's departure. Sport throws up some strange ironies.

Maurice now had the awesome task of getting the international team back on the road. Rod McKenzie had already been offered a new contract as fitness consultant to the Rugby Football League. One of the first decisions that Maurice made was to enlist the support and assistance of Phil Larder, the National Director of Coaching. This was a far-sighted decision which not only reflected great credit on Maurice, but was to be a long-term benefit to both international preparation and Rugby League in general.

Prior to 1982 relationships between the Rugby Football League and the British Amateur Rugby League Association were strained to say the least. BARLA had been granted independence in 1973 and was given a mandate by the RFL to take total responsibility for the promotion and development of amateur rugby. Pressure for change had come about because of the neglect of the RFL council who, for a variety of reasons, had devoted most of its energy and resources to ensure the survival of the professional game. Regrettably, the council had become inward-looking and had failed to grasp a fundamental principle, that is, that the game of Rugby League needed to be strong at all levels – not only the professional clubs, but also the schools, the amateur clubs and, in a few short years, universities and colleges. The opportunity to establish an overall development policy for the game which embraced the needs of the amateurs was ignored, and I suspect there was a sigh of relief from the RFL when it granted BARLA its independence.

When the amateurs, with some financial support from the RFL, had received control of their own destiny they tackled the job of setting up committees, writing a new constitution, creating league structures and a hundred and one other related tasks with clear determination. Inevitably the division between BARLA and the RFL widened and the main battleground was youth rugby. BARLA wanted total responsibility for developing youth rugby and accused the RFL of sabotaging their efforts at expansion by continuing to support an Under-19 competition for the professional clubs. The RFL were equally adamant that the survival of the professional clubs depended upon their having their own nursery of young players.

A decade of rivalry and friction between the RFL and BARLA proved costly in terms of player development. Australia had no such conflict; there, under one governing body, there was one overall Rugby League development policy which embraced all facets of the game. Professional clubs in Sydney were required to support amateur clubs and schoolboy teams with finance and a development and coaching scheme. The outstanding Australian Test teams of 1982 and 1984 were a product of a coherent system which focused on the 9-year-old as much as the adult: one game, one governing body.

In 1982 the RFL and BARLA came together and agreed that Rugby League's National Coaching Scheme was in need of major reform and that the dedicated work of Laurie Gant and Albert Fearnley, under the direction of Bill Fallowfield, a former secretary of the Rugby Football League, needed to be extended and developed if it was to produce the quantity and quality of coaches necessary for the expansion of Rugby League. The scheme was also to take account of the needs of the professional game, as it was mistakenly believed that professional coaches were born, not made. The skills necessary to survive at professional level are varied, and being an ex-international with a strong personality is not the be-all and end-all of the job. The modern coach needs to develop a knowledge of organisation, administration, public relations and counselling, as well as fitness training and skills development. Australian coaches are expected to have attended coaching courses arranged by the Australian Rugby League and to have gained recognised qualifications. Not only was Australia producing a different breed of player in the 1980s, it was also producing a different breed of coach.

In the reorganisation of the coaching scheme early in 1982 Phil Larder was appointed National Director of Coaching. He set about the task of reform with the determination and professionalism that became the hallmarks of his success. He spent a great deal of time studying the methods of Frank Stanton and the 1982 Kangaroos, and constructed the courses of the coaching scheme so that the lessons of the Test series might be learned and never need to be taught again. However, many established coaches resented his intrusion into the professional game and either ignored his efforts or despised them in these early years. But Maurice Bamford recognised Phil Larder's qualities, and his appointment as assistant coach to the Great Britain team in 1984 gave him both the credibility he needed and a platform from which to project the work of the National Coaching Scheme. If Larder's work was the only point on which the RFL and BARLA had agreed in ten years, it was perhaps the most significant bridgehead for the future of the game that they could have established.

The position of Great Britain manager was not considered until February 1985. Once again, I was keen to fill the post which, this time, was properly advertised. Candidates were invited to submit their curriculum vitae with a copy available for each council member.

I was born in the small industrial town of Millom in south Cumberland and, as a boy, had been brought up watching Barrow when the club resumed playing after the Second World War. The Barrow team contained the legendary Willie Horne who demonstrated extraordinary skills as a stand-off,

Phil Jackson and Denis Goodwin, flying wingers Jimmie Lewthwaite and Frank Castle, and forwards Jack Grundy and Reg Parker. It was this successful team that captured my youthful imagination and inspired me to play the game of Rugby League myself.

As I grew older, I captained my school at Rugby Union on Saturday mornings and turned out for Millom Rugby League in the Barrow and District League on Saturday afternoons. During my final year at school I was invited for trials with Workington Town by their player-coach, the legendary Gus Risman. Gus was keen to sign me, but with national service coming up and college after that I was advised by my parents to postpone any ideas of professional rugby for a year or two. Gus kept track of my progress, however, and when I was selected for the Cumberland Rugby Union squad he asked me if I was still keen to fulfil my ambition to play professional Rugby League. I had a successful trial with Salford, where Gus was now the manager, and I signed professional terms in March 1957. Although I never became an international I played 330 first-team games for Salford and represented Cumberland on several occasions.

I retired from playing in 1970 and Brian Snape, the club chairman, appointed me assistant coach to Cliff Evans, the former Swinton and St Helens coach. Salford had a host of outstanding and classy players in the 1970s, including Paul Charlton, Keith Fielding, Chris Hesketh, David Watkins, Ken Gill, Steve Nash, Maurice Richards, Mike Coulman and Colin Dixon – a real who's who of RL. Following Cliff Evans's retirement I fulfilled my ambition to become coach, and in 1974 and 1976 Salford won the first-division Championship.

In 1977 I stepped down from my position as coach and was invited by Brian Snape to join the board of directors. Brian Snape was not only an outstanding club chairman, he also filled the position of chairman of the Rugby Football League with great distinction. He was a man with imagination and vision, and those who came into contact with him were soon impressed with his ideas for the promotion and expansion of Rugby League. In 1978 he retired to the Isle of Man, and the game lost a man it could ill afford to lose. I replaced him on the Rugby Football League council as member for Salford, serving on the international selection committee and filling the post of chairman of the coaching committee. By 1985 I was not only an experienced member of the council but believed myself highly qualified to fill the position of Great Britain manager.

When I arrived at Rugby Football League HQ in Leeds for the interview for the position of Great Britain manager, I found that my rivals included Bob Ashby of Featherstone, Maurice Lindsay of Wigan, Phil Brunt of Castleford and Reg Parker of Blackpool. All were capable and influential men within the game; Reg Parker was in fact a former tour manager, and the others were successful club chairmen. If I was to succeed I had to get it right when I appeared in front of the Rugby Football League council.

Appearing in front of over thirty council members is a daunting prospect.

But I had lived with the ambition of being Great Britain manager for some time and I genuinely believed that I had the necessary qualifications to fulfil the role. I entered the council chamber confidently, and outlined our current international standing, put forward reasons for this decline and presented the necessary strategy for change and why I was the man to effect that change. I concluded by saying, 'We can't afford to fail, gentlemen – this time the whole of Rugby League demands that we get it right.' At the end of the interview the council discussed the various presentations while we candidates waited for the decision.

When we were called back into the council chamber, Joe Seddon of St Helens, the chairman, thanked us all for our applications, complimented us on our interviews and then said, 'The council is pleased to appoint Les Bettinson manager of the Great Britain team.' I thanked the council for its confidence and assured everyone that I would not fail. I felt enormously proud as members shook my hand and wished me well, although I knew that I was going to need all my experience to fulfil the role of manager and it was by no means going to be a bed of roses.

I now had to put words into action, and what I needed to do was to meet Maurice Bamford, the coach. I arranged to meet with Maurice at the George Hotel, Huddersfield, for lunch two days later. I was a little apprehensive about the meeting as I knew that some of my quotes in the newspapers, given when I was in a state of euphoria, may have given Maurice the wrong impression. I had talked of the changes I would make, referring, of course, to previous management regimes and not to any of the changes that Maurice had already introduced. In the cold light of day, however, it seemed that I had implied criticism of current arrangements; that was certainly not my intention.

We shook hands and expressed the usual pleasantries. Initially Maurice was rather guarded, but as we talked about Rugby League we soon began to relax. By the time we sat down for lunch we knew that we would become good friends and that the friendship would continue long after we had ceased to be manager and coach of Great Britain.

The big challenge facing Great Britain was the advent of the Kiwi tourists in the autumn of 1985. More immediately pressing, however, were the two Tests against France in March for which Maurice had already selected a squad. The squad was strongly criticised as Maurice had deliberately left out many leading players from the 1984 tour. Missing were Andy Gregory, Tony Myler, Lee Crooks, Mick Burke, Garry Schofield and Joe Lydon. Maurice explained that he wanted to blood some new players and that this was the only opportunity he would get. He also wanted to create a new team spirit, a new attitude, a new pride, and he was concerned that some of the old guard might prevent that from happening. His enthusiasm for the task ahead was infectious and the players responded quickly to his warm personality. He had a natural ability to communicate and saw humour in every situation. However, players who cheated or showed a poor attitude soon felt the sharp edge of his tongue. Maurice had presence and his training sessions and meetings reflected that. He made things happen.

My first objective as the new manager was to gain Maurice's trust. When we went into camp the day before the Headingley Test match, I consciously maintained a low profile and kept from under his feet, although I attended the training sessions, sat in meetings and played in the snooker competition. Yet Maurice's generosity of spirit was overwhelming. He deliberately set out to reinforce my position by inviting me to express an opinion or view to the players whenever possible, and he prefaced all of his talks by saying 'the manager and I believe'. The trust that developed between us became an essential ingredient in Maurice's concept of the Great Britain team as 'the family'.

When Maurice and I led the team out at Headingley on the evening of Friday 1 March 1985 I felt choked and my eyes were more than a little misty. It was a very powerful, emotional experience which took me by surprise,

Les Bettinson and Maurice Bamford began their partnership at the helm of the national side with a record win over France. A fortnight later they came crashing back down to earth in the return match at Perpignan.

but it was nothing compared to the elation I felt after the game. The result exceeded our wildest expectations with a record 50–4 victory.

The team included no less than nine new caps, and every man had reason to be proud of his performance. Roy Dickinson, Alan Rathbone and David Watkinson grafted long and hard in the face of an uncompromising French pack, allowing Andy Goodway and Ellery Hanley to confirm the good impressions they had made in Australia, and Gary Divorty and Deryck Fox to carve up the midfield. Both of these youngsters scored début tries, as did Vince Gribbin, earning praise for completing a successful transition from second division to Test football. David Creasser marked his first appearance with eight goals, while Shaun Edwards overcame a nervous start to put in a solid display at full-back. Maurice's young team showed an insatiable appetite for point-scoring, and it was difficult to believe that his selectorial policy had not been absolutely right.

Great Britain: Edwards (Wigan); Ledger (St Helens), Creasser (Leeds), Gribbin (Whitehaven), Gill (Wigan); Hanley (Bradford Northern), Fox (Featherstone Rovers); Dickinson (Leeds), Watkinson (Hull KR), Dannatt (Hull), Goodway (Oldham), Rathbone (Bradford Northern), Divorty (Hull)
Substitutes: Gibson (Batley) for Gill after 51 minutes; Platt (St Helens) not used
Scorers: tries – Hanley (2), Fox (2), Gill, Watkinson, Gribbin, Divorty; goals – Creasser (8), Fox

France: Pallarès; Jean, Palisses, Fourquet, Ratier; Perez, Grésèque; Chantal, Macalli, Meurin, Aillères, Guy Laforgue, Dominic Baloup
Substitutes: Bergé for Meurin after 56 minutes; Francis Laforgue not used
Scorer: try – Macalli

Referee: B. Gomersall (Australia)

Keith Macklin of *The Times* wrote, 'There have been so many false dawns in the past decade that to read too much into Great Britain's 50–4 win would be foolishly premature. However, only three hours before the spectacularly unexpected Headingley win I had chatted to Maurice Bamford and Les Bettinson at their Garforth hotel and both had stressed that a win over France, by whatever margin, would be merely the beginning. Brave words had been spoken before but Messrs Bamford and Bettinson, backed up by the National Director of Coaching, Phil Larder, stressed that any long term success by Great Britain would depend on total commitment at club level, amateur level, colts and youth level and in the schools.'

Ray French, writing in the *Rugby Leaguer*, saw it as a 'welcome light at the end of the long dark tunnel'. His match report included: 'The fact that

I, and no doubt many others, disagreed with more than half of the Great Britain selections didn't matter. For I think, and I hope, that I have seen a distinct change of heart for the better. I could sense that the preparation of the squad had been first-class, that discipline on and off the field had been instilled into the side by the enthusiasm and obvious dedication of both Bamford and Bettinson.'

Maurice had originally selected a Test squad featuring sixteen new caps, and had given his word that all members of the squad would play in one

Phil Ford was one of the few pluses to emerge from the defeat at Perpignan in March 1985. As an elusive yet unpredictable runner, he delighted and frustrated spectators throughout the late 1980s.

or other of the French matches. Consequently we travelled to Perpignan for the return match with a side showing eight changes, but team spirit was high and the preparations had gone well. On the morning of the match, however, the team captain, Andy Goodway, went down with flu and had to withdraw. He was replaced with Andy Dannatt, and Ellery Hanley assumed the captaincy for the first time.

It was not an auspicious start for Hanley. A similarly restructured French team played with much greater panache and determination, and had established a 24–6 lead by half-time. The new left winger, Didier Couston, notched a hat-trick in a devastating twenty-minute spell, two of the tries resulting from interceptions of passes thrown by Hanley and

Divorty. Although Hanley led a spirited second-half rally that clawed back 10 points, the arrears were too much for Great Britain to overhaul. There was satisfaction only in the performances of Phil Ford, who scored two tries on his international début and always looked dangerous, and Paul Harkin, a second-half substitute for the disappointing Deryck Fox.

France: Pallarès; Ratier, Fourquet, Palisses, Couston; Francis Laforgue, Grésèque; Chantal, Macalli, Titeux, Montgaillard, Verdes, Guy Laforgue
Substitutes: Mendes for Palisses after 36 minutes, Bernabé for Mendes after 68 minutes
Scorers: tries – Couston (3), Fourquet; goals – Pallarès (4)

Great Britain: Johnson (Leigh); Clark (Hull KR), Creasser (Leeds), Foy (Oldham), Phil Ford (Wigan); Hanley (Bradford Northern), Fox (Featherstone Rovers); Dickinson (Leeds), Kiss (Wigan), Wane (Wigan), Dannatt (Hull), Rathbone (Bradford Northern), Divorty (Hull)
Substitutes: Harkin (Hull KR) for Fox after 40 minutes, Roy Powell (Leeds) for Dickinson after 56 minutes
Scorers: tries – Phil Ford (2), Foy; goals – Creasser, Divorty

Referee: B. Gomersall (Australia)

In two weeks Maurice and I had experienced the joy of victory and the despair of defeat, and we knew which one we liked best. We also knew the scale of the task facing us. The Headingley Test had shown that we were working with some promising – in some cases, outstanding – material; Perpignan showed that some players were either not good enough or not yet ready for Test football. Yet we knew we were on the right lines; surely, now, British Rugby League was ready to turn the corner.

2

...g on the Kiwis

...rly in June 1985 the RFL agreed to send an international team to Limoux to play a French President's XIII in a match to commemorate the death of two French sportswriters, Alex Angel and Guy Cassayet. Not every leading player was available, but we were able to assemble a pretty useful squad for what was to prove an invaluable part of our preparations for the visit of the Kiwis. It not only provided an additional opportunity to work with potential Test players but it also enabled Maurice Bamford, Phil Larder and myself to get to know each other and to experiment with one or two ideas.

Phil Larder had visited Australia the previous year and spent some time with Jack Gibson, the legendary coach of Cronulla. On his return Phil had produced a detailed report for the Rugby Football League which isolated the four key areas that a team needs to emphasise in order to succeed: control of the game, the kicking game, defence, and support play.

To control a game a team needs to keep possession of the ball for six tackles, which requires considerable concentration, commitment and discipline. Position on the pitch is crucial; to gain a good position a team needs a strategy that involves varied and intelligent kicking of the ball in both attack and defence. Defence is also vital and needs to be practised at every training session, with particular emphasis on defence around the play-the-ball. Support play is the fourth component of success, and this requires skill and fitness. In the hot French sunshine of Limoux Maurice and Phil coached the players in these four areas, and team meetings reinforced the overall game plan. The end result was an easy victory for the British XIII, with Ellery Hanley scoring five times and John Fieldhouse and Ian Potter giving notice of the forces they were to become in Test football.

The following day Maurice convened a team meeting, and each player was asked to pinpoint two areas of his game he was pleased with and one area he needed to work on. The session was very enlightening, revealed the basic honesty of the players, and was to prove a vital part of player education. Indeed, the whole exercise in Limoux was most instructive, with Maurice and Phil demonstrating a great capacity to learn new things and to experiment. The players in turn responded because they knew that

Maurice cared for them and was passionately proud of his position as Great Britain coach.

During the rest of the summer a training-on squad met at Carnegie College for fitness training under Rod McKenzie and skills training under Maurice and Phil. This originally comprised a total of thirty-seven players, although five, Goodway, Schofield, Crooks, Harkin and Noble, opted to spend the summer playing in Australia. Tony Myler and Andy Gregory, for business reasons, and Garry Clark, pleading fatigue, asked to be excused; they received pretty short shrift from Maurice.

Maurice himself travelled to Australia and New Zealand to attend the trans-Tasman Test matches. He returned with great respect for Graham Lowe's emerging Kiwis, who lost the series to a last-minute try by Australia's John Ribot. Lowe was destined to achieve immortality as the coach of Wigan, and was a keen student of all aspects of his job, team-work, man-management and psychology. In one area he was definitely further down the road then we were, and that was in knowing his best team – because it was tried and tested and because he had developed a special relationship of trust with his players. Those players included the imposing captain, Mark Graham, Kevin and Howie Tamati, Kurt and Dane Sorensen, James Leuleuai, Clayton Friend and Hugh McGahan – all formidable players, and we had to find players capable of matching them every step of the way.

The 1985 New Zealand tourists provided formidable opposition for Great Britain, holding them to a drawn series. Their traditional *haka* was used as a psychological weapon both on and off the field.

We had approval from the RFL management board to take a squad of twenty-six players to the National Sports Centre at Lilleshall in Shropshire for several days preparation. This had been planned to the last detail and was designed above all else to develop team spirit. The players were divided into four teams for the week and had to take part in a series of competitions including games, relays, races, tackling circuits and so on. Imagine my

horror, therefore, when I observed three members of the press striding across the field to see what the new Great Britain preparation was all about – at the precise moment when the teams were lining up for the sack race, to be followed by the egg-and-spoon race. This was a light-hearted diversion taken very seriously by the players – after all, a competition is a competition – but I am not sure to this day how Peter Wilson of the *Daily Star* regarded it. Peter had been very critical of the organisation of the 1984 tour and had regaled me with horror stories about the Great Britain team going to training sessions without practice balls and not turning up to civic receptions. When I told him that the players also had to produce a concert as part of the week's competition he wrote it down, but I am not sure he believed me.

The week was a huge success as the players worked hard and did everything asked of them. They completed a questionnaire designed by a sports psychologist to provide additional information which could be useful to us in team preparation. One of the questions asked them to write down the name of the player they most admired or respected. Harry Pinner came top of the list, and this was an important consideration in his eventual appointment as captain of Great Britain for the Kiwi series.

It was at Lilleshall that Sully the lion came into being. Maurice believed that the New Zealand players had a greater pride in playing for their country than ours, and that this pride gave the Kiwis their competitive edge. The New Zealanders always carried a toy Kiwi to training and to matches as a symbol of their patriotism. Our players agreed with Maurice that Great Britain should adopt a lion, to be christened Sully after Clive Sullivan, the former Great Britain captain who had recently died of cancer. Mick Burke, the Widnes full-back, came up with the idea of the players holding a Union Jack during the national anthem, and the players responded to this with enthusiasm. Maurice asked them to keep the idea secret until the day of the first Test.

We left Lilleshall in high spirits for the three warm-up games the following week against Oldham, Hull KR and Cumbria, which ended in two conclusive victories and a draw. We then sat down to select the team for the first Test. Although Maurice now had the sole power of selection he never exercised that right but preferred to arrive at decisions by consensus. If it came to a difference of opinion over the merits of a particular player then we would debate it further to see if the difference could be resolved. In the end Maurice, of course, had the casting vote. The procedure for selection was always the same throughout my time as manager. It involved Maurice, Phil and myself naming players who were in contention for each position; generally, there was considerable agreement. We would then debate why certain players had been included in the list, analyse their relative strengths and experience, check match reports and previous records and so carry out a process of elimination. Club form was important, but we always valued personal character, attitude in training, ability to cope with stress, big-match temperament, personality, and whether or not they were 'winners'. We had also to bear in mind the likely tactics or game plan to be adopted, for which the players best suited would be selected.

Once the team was selected we moved into camp at the luxurious Shaw Hill hotel–cum–golf complex at Chorley, owned by Denis Rodin of Wigan, whose company sponsored the annual challenge match between Lancashire and Yorkshire. He had arranged for the management and staff of the hotel to do everything possible to ensure that we were given first-class treatment, and Shaw Hill was to become the permanent home for all our international preparations in the years to come. This had a tremendous psychological effect on the players, who realised that international selection had become a privilege and that their status was reflected in the way they were treated and looked after. Their personal comforts were given absolute priority, with meals being of an exceptional quality. Prawn cocktails have always been the players' favourite, but the chef took a personal interest in ensuring variety and quality. Rice puddings, pasta and bread pudding were included in the diet to maintain a high level of carbohydrates.

Maurice and Phil prepared training sessions down to the last detail and these were reinforced with team meetings which analysed videos of New Zealand's matches, identified key players and laid down our game plan. Maurice used those meetings to build up his personal rapport with the players, and generate a family spirit which we hoped would forge a winning team. In between Maurice organised snooker competitions and sports quizzes, and presided over everything like a benevolent father.

We left for the first Test at Headingley on 19 October in confident mood. As we travelled over the Pennines the final motivation for the players was to watch a video specially prepared by Phil which featured all of them making excellent runs or tackles in recent matches. The 1982 Kangaroos had watched *Rocky* and *Chariots of Fire* for similar effect; it was a lesson worth absorbing.

When Maurice and I led the team out we both had immense feelings of pride and anticipation: had we got it right? The pre-match formalities took place and then, as the band played the national anthem, the crowd rose to the Great Britain team when they formed a circle, linked arms and held the Union Jack. At the end of the anthem two players ran to the popular side with the flag waving proudly between them. It was unashamed patriotic jingoism but it had an electrifying effect.

Andy Goodway got Great Britain away to a dream start by claiming a scrambled touchdown after the stand-in Kiwi full-back, James Leuleuai, dropped a high kick by Harry Pinner. However, once Pinner had been sized up and closed down by the New Zealand defence, the majestic Mark Graham led a surge that took the Kiwis into a 14–6 lead with three tries in quick succession. However, Graham sustained a painful ankle injury, and while he was receiving treatment, Ellery Hanley brought Great Britain back into the match with a typical solo effort. Graham was unable to continue

Ellery Hanley shows an early glimpse of his rare try-scoring ability as he dives over between the posts to bring Great Britain back into contention in the first Test against New Zealand at Headingley in 1985.

after half-time, and control of the play fluctuated until Des Drummond broke from his own line, passed infield to the substitute, Arkwright, who fed Hanley, and Hanley stormed away up the touchline before looping a pass inside to Joe Lydon for the try. It was a score fit to win any match, but with just seconds remaining Dane O'Hara ran back a loose clearing kick, found Gary Prohm who in turn found Kurt Sorensen, and the giant forward reached round the back of a defender to put Leuleuai in under the posts. Filipaina converted to win a breathtaking match for New Zealand by 24–22.

Great Britain: Burke (Widnes); Drummond (Leigh), Schofield (Hull), Hanley (Wigan), Lydon (Widnes); Tony Myler (Widnes), Fox (Featherstone Rovers); Crooks (Hull), Watkinson (Hull KR), Fieldhouse (Widnes), Goodway (Wigan), Potter (Wigan), Pinner (St Helens)
Substitutes: Arkwright (St Helens) for Crooks after 55 minutes; David

Hulme (Widnes) not used
Scorers: tries – Goodway, Hanley, Lydon; goals – Burke (3), Lydon
(2)

New Zealand: Leuleuai; Bell, Ah Kuoi, Prohm, O'Hara; Filipaina,
Friend; Kurt Sorensen, Howie Tamati, Dane Sorensen, Graham, Wright,
McGahan
Substitutes: Kemble for Ah Kuoi after 40 minutes, Kevin Tamati for
Graham after 41 minutes
Scorers: tries – O'Hara, Bell, Graham, Kurt Sorensen, Leuleuai; goals –
Filipaina (2)

Referee: B. Gomersall (Australia)

I trudged off the field feeling cheated and emotionally drained. At that
moment months of hard work appeared to have gone up in smoke. In the
dressing-room the players were defiant and shouts of 'We'll do the bastards
next time' echoed round the room. One player who took the defeat very
personally was Andy Goodway, who had had an indifferent game by his
own high standards and judged himself harshly. 'Don't select me again,'
he said to me as he hurried from the dressing-room. This destructive
side of Andy's personality was a real handicap to his international career;
he psyched himself up to play well and if he failed to deliver by his
standards he suffered inevitable depression. We asked his club to talk
him round.

The media reaction after the match was very encouraging; newspaper
headlines read 'Britain Find Their Pride', 'We Want Revenge', and 'Britain
Back In Business'. The match had been an exciting contest with excellent
tries from both sides; although we had lost, the verdict was that Rugby
League had won in front of a sizeable TV audience. Here, if anywhere, was
the precise point where the start of our road to international recovery can
be recognised, even though there were still to be set-backs along the way.

Our post mortem was reassuring, too. In the main our selection had
been spot on. John Fieldhouse, a controversial selection as a prop, won
the man-of-the-match award, and Deryck Fox at scrum-half did more than
enough to justify his position above Andy Gregory. Our defence was not as
tight as it should have been, and we still lagged behind the excellent Kiwis
in our support play, but overall we emerged with credit.

For the second Test we had to find a replacement for Lee Crooks
who had been forced to leave the field at Headingley with concussion.
Maurice had no hesitation in recalling Jeff Grayshon, then of Leeds, to
the international scene, even though he was a veteran of 36 and had been
part of the humiliated Great Britain team in 1982.

During the preparations for the second Test the players kidded Jeff about
his antiquity and offered him Phyllosan and Horlicks at bed-time. He took

it all in his stride, and his dedication made an enormous impression on the squad; we knew that he would not let himself or his country down, despite the reservations of informed press opinion.

As we arrived at Wigan on Saturday 2 November confirmation that Mark Graham, the New Zealand captain, had failed a fitness test gave us a last-minute boost. Maurice went about the final stages of preparation with a calmness that belied the emotion he was feeling. As the Great Britain coach he had moved away from his fire-and-brimstone team-talk, preferring to move around quietly advising each player and reminding them of what he expected from them. Ten minutes from kick-off he went through the tactical game plan for the final time, but the look in the eyes of the players reassured him that they were ready.

Great Britain's performance was a revelation, and Maurice's confidence in his game plan and in the players' ability to interpret it was fully justified. Jeff Grayshon's contribution close to the ruck allowed Harry Pinner to stand that much wider to work off the excellent Deryck Fox and feed the powerful runs of Myler and Hanley. But it was Garry Schofield who stole the headlines with an astonishing exhibition of support play that saw him sprint in for four tries to equal Billy Boston's 21-year-old Test record. Their preparations blighted by injury and ill fortune, the Kiwis were torn to pieces by the young centre. Graham Lowe made no excuses: 'The way we played today, the Blind Institute would have beaten us.'

Great Britian: Burke (Widnes); Drummond (Leigh), Schofield (Hull), Hanley (Wigan), Lydon (Widnes); Tony Myler (Widnes), Fox (Featherstone Rovers); Grayshon (Leeds), Watkinson (Hull KR), Fieldhouse (Widnes), Goodway (Wigan), Potter (Wigan), Pinner (St Helens)
Substitutes: Edwards (Wigan) for Burke after 42 minutes, Burton (Hull KR) for Goodway after 55 minutes
Scorers: tries – Schofield (4); goals – Lydon (4); drop-goal – Pinner

New Zealand: Kemble; Bell, Leuleuai, Prohm, O'Hara; Filipaina, Friend; Kurt Sorensen, Howie Tamati, Dane Sorensen, West, Stewart, McGahan
Substitutes: Ah Kuoi for West after 46 minutes, Cowan for Stewart after 70 minutes
Scorers: try – Bell; goals – Filipaina (2)

Referee: B. Gomersall (Australia)

Opposite Deryck Fox earned his international jersey in 1985 and 1986, ahead of such rivals as Andy Gregory, for his non-stop work rate, calm organisation and effective kicking game.

The press flocked into the cramped Central Park dressing-room as the champagne flowed to celebrate the end of a run of ten successive defeats by Australia and New Zealand. Paul Fitzpatrick of the *Guardian* encapsulated the relief of all involved with British Rugby League when he wrote: 'The age of disillusionment ended at Central Park, Wigan, on Saturday when Great Britain not only beat New Zealand but did so with style and conviction. Now under the guidance of the most thorough management team the national side has possibly ever known, Great Britain have a future again'. Although we were not carried away by the victory we certainly enjoyed the reflected glory and we felt that our approach was the right one.

For the deciding Test at Leeds we included Lee Crooks as substitute and retained Jeff Grayshon, but at the eleventh hour we were forced

to make a crucial change. I had not been present at the final training
session on the Friday and when I met the team off the coach at Shaw
Hill Maurice's grim look told me that there was a problem. Tony Myler
had pulled a hamstring. Over lunch we decided not to release the news
to the press until the day of the match but we would have an emergency
meeting of the players immediately and clear up any doubts or speculation
by ruling Tony out there and then. We would move Hanley to stand-off and
play Shaun Edwards at centre. We felt that by being positive in this way we
would minimise the shock of losing Tony.

At the age of 36, veteran prop Jeff Grayshon was recalled to the national colours for the second and third Kiwi Tests of 1985 following an injury to Lee Crooks.

There was one more crisis before we took the field on Saturday 9
November and even now I break out in a cold sweat thinking about it.
Although we left for Elland Road in good time we ran into roadworks
on the M62 and soon found ourselves in the middle of a long tailback.
It didn't take a genius to calculate that at the rate we were moving we
would not get to Elland Road in time for the match. Now breaking the
law is not something I would normally contemplate, but without hesitation
I ordered the reluctant driver to drive up the hard shoulder. This he did
until we came to a substantial stretch of motorway that was marked out

of bounds by bollards – by then it was 'devil take the hindmost'. I jumped from the coach, moved some bollards and cleared the way for the driver to progress in style down an empty road. Motorway workers waved at us – at least I think they were waving – but we forged ahead and arrived at Elland Road at 2:15, forty-five minutes before kick-off and half an hour later then we had anticipated.

Although we were keyed up for victory, New Zealand were not above a little psychological warfare under the shrewd eye of Graham Lowe. Just before kick-off the Kiwis came into the corridor outside our dressing-room to perform their *haka* with the express purpose of unnerving us. As the primeval sound echoed around it certainly had an effect on us, but only to stiffen the sinews. Out on the pitch we smiled to see that for their national anthem the Kiwis had found a New Zealand flag, and every Kiwi in Britain must have stood in the circle round it as they sang.

Public interest in the match was phenomenal, attracted by the standard of the fare served up in the first two Tests, but in view of some of the unsavoury incidents that blighted the decider that interest seemed something of a two-edged sword. With ten changes from the line-up fielded at Wigan, New Zealand followed up their psychological onslaught with a defensive display of bloodcurdling and often illegal ferocity. The net result of this was the departure of Andy Goodway, with concussion, and of Kurt Sorensen, to the sin bin, after twenty-five minutes. By that stage Mark Graham, fit again to lead his side, had taken advantage of a defensive slip to go over the line from the play-the-ball and give New Zealand a 6–0 lead at the interval.

It was only an interception by Des Drummond that prevented the Kiwis extending their lead after half-time, but still they were conceding penalties at a frightening rate. It was from two of these that Lee Crooks, on for Goodway, brought Great Britain back to 6–4. Tempers continued to run high and, as a scrum erupted in a mass brawl and referee Gomersall looked on helplessly, it was left to two policemen to enter the field of play and separate the fighting players. Finally, two minutes from time, a dangerous tackle by Gary Prohm out on the touchline gave Crooks one last chance to level the scores. From his 'wrong' side, with the hopes of the nation resting on his shoulders, he did not miss, and the series was shared.

Great Britain: Burke (Widnes); Drummond (Leigh), Schofield (Hull), Edwards (Wigan), Lydon (Widnes); Hanley (Wigan), Fox (Featherstone Rovers); Grayshon (Leeds), Watkinson (Hull KR), Fieldhouse (Widnes), Goodway (Wigan), Potter (Wigan), Pinner (St Helens)
Substitutes: Crooks (Hull) for Goodway after 25 minutes, Arkwright (St Helens) after Watkinson for 64 minutes
Scorers: goals – Crooks (3)

New Zealand: Kemble; Williams, Bell, Leuleuai, O'Hara; Ah Kuoi, Friend; Kevin Tamati, Wallace, Dane Sorensen, Graham, Kurt Sorensen, Prohm

Substitutes: Filipaina for Ah Kuoi after 73 minutes, McGahan for Kevin Tamati after 73 minutes

Scorers: try – Graham; goal – Dane Sorensen

Referee: B. Gomersall (Australia)

Lee Crooks launches the penalty goal that drew both the third Kiwi Test and the series in 1985. The Great Britain bench adopt a variety of disinterested poses in the background.

Ian Wooldridge of the *Daily Mail* had travelled north to see the deciding Test match because he had been impressed with the re-emergence of British Rugby League in the previous Tests. The match may have disappointed him as a classic encounter of free-flowing rugby but he saw plenty to write about.

'There were moments – I lie, there were whole extended instalments – when the third Test resembled nothing less than the house party the Campbells gave for the Macdonalds.' He went on to describe in similarly graphic style the performance of the referee: 'In an area of the ground well out of the cross-fire stood the referee, Australia's Barry Gomersall. He was flapping his arms about like an apprentice chaplain caught in a riot at

Wormwood Scrubs high security wing. I know nothing about Rugby League but I have seen a lot of referees in one sport or another and Mr Gomersall, on Saturday's performance, does not figure in the first five thousand.' Even allowing for Wooldridge's poetic licence it was perhaps a little exaggerated, yet the brawl was what the press focused on. It was publicity of the worst conceivable kind.

Wooldridge did compliment Rugby League supporters, however, when he wrote, 'It isn't true, by the way, that violence on the field induces violence on the terraces. The 22,000 in the ground were impeccably behaved. The other phenomenon was the staggering absence of any acrimony between the two teams afterwards.' What also surprised him was the open access of our dressing-room to the press immediately after the match, by comparison with soccer which has long since closed its doors.

Jack McNamara, a long-serving Rugby League writer with the *Manchester Evening News*, described Maurice and me as 'an unlikely combination at first glance: Bettinson the polished senior education adviser for Stockport; Bamford a joiner by trade and bluff, archetypal Yorkshireman by nature. But they, along with Phil Larder, have worked well together.'

I had tried hard to establish a pattern of working together which relied on trust, consensus, negotiation and consistency. My temperament is less suited to the conflict and high drama which some managers and coaches appear to thrive on. I rely heavily on treating people with respect and sensitivity; it is a management style concentrating largely on inter-personal skills. But politeness and diplomacy should never mean compromising one's principles, although compromise in human interaction is more likely to succeed than confrontation.

When I became coach to Salford in the 1973–74 season I was asked by the press how I would cope with handling so many international players when I had never been an international myself. The answer was that my relationship with players at Salford succeeded because I worked at it. Organisation and communication were my priorities, and these need to be of a high order in any organisation if it is to prosper. Training sessions at Salford were well organised and carried out with efficiency. Players had a high expectation when they arrived for team preparation and this was fulfilled. Team-work was the essence of my particular approach, and involving players in decision-making, particularly about tactics, paid dividends. These were the management principles I brought with me to the Great Britain management team.

Maurice had not had the opportunity for further education once he left school, and had to acquire his skills and style as a coach from whatever source was available. His passion for the game and thirst for knowledge were insatiable; he read widely and debated coaching strategies with anyone whom he thought had something to offer. With extraordinary honesty Maurice would talk about his 'dinosaur' period when he believed that coaching was about passion, fire-and-brimstone motivational tirades and fear. Over the years he realised that coaching is more than that, and that treating players as individuals is so much more important.

Jack McNamara was right. On the face of it we were an unlikely pair, but our love of Rugby League, its history and its culture meant that we talked a common language, and together we became a formidable combination. He was an extrovert; I more of an introvert. He could be volatile; I was more stable. He had a gambler's instinct; I was more cautious. By a strange chemistry we complemented each other very well.

Rival captains Harry Pinner of Great Britain (left) and Mark Graham of New Zealand, along with third Test hero Lee Crooks, show the trophy that they shared with the 1985 Test series.

The final verdict on the progress we had made in 1985 came from Ray French in the *Rugby Leaguer*: 'From the time when the players in open session were asked to criticise themselves before their team-mates, throughout the coaching sessions where great attention was paid to individual strengths and weaknesses, to the absorbing meetings where, with the help of specially prepared tapes, the team's performance was analysed, the whole programme smacked of sheer professionalism. The relationship between management and players was one of relaxed respect, and rarely have I heard players more articulate in expressing positive points of view. I came away more heartened than I have ever done from a British training camp in the last five years. We are on the right lines at last; please let no one derail us.'

3

Revolution and a Recce

It was early in 1986 that the prospect of a 'Super League' breakaway became a serious threat and caused shockwaves throughout the game. The idea had been mooted for some time, and certainly club chairmen such as Maurice Lindsay of Wigan and Roy Waudby of Hull were open advocates. They and others believed that the game was, if not stagnating, at least being held back by unambitious second-division clubs who were happy to be subsidised by the more successful first-division clubs paying 15 per cent of their gross earnings to the Rugby Football League for redistribution. However, reformers were handicapped by the constitution which required a two-thirds majority before any by-law could be changed. Conservatives such as Jack Grindrod of Rochdale openly stated that the 15 per cent levy was a trade-off negotiated by the clubs when the two-division structure came into being in 1973, and that first-division clubs should not now try to renege on that agreement.

The Rugby Football League council was, in 1986, a fascinating organisation made up of thirty-five club representatives, often strong personalities with little in common, controlled by David Oxley, then secretary-general, and an annually elected chairman. Its bible was the black book containing the by-laws; steering successfully through those was a major challenge. Two large sub-committees conducted some of the business but the main policy-making body was the full council. Effecting significant change in such an unwieldy body was very difficult and required a combination of statesmanship, strong personality, plotting in small sub-groups and unashamed lobbying. When the council agreed to elect a nine-man management board in 1983 in an effort to streamline the business of the council it was, in retrospect, an open admission of frustration and a vote for common sense.

In 1986 I was chairman of a small committee with responsibility for controlling and improving coaching. We had taken it upon ourselves to draw up a development plan for the game as a whole; although it was well outside our brief, nevertheless we were prepared to identify key issues which we felt that the council should address. It seemed that the management board was getting bogged down with day-to-day matters and was reduced to fire-fighting, whereas the council only met every two months and was overwhelmed with inertia. Short- or long-term planning was very difficult, but David Oxley, who also sat on the coaching committee, welcomed the ideas we were discussing because they were fundamentally about improving the quality of Rugby League at all levels – coaching, playing, development, marketing and administration.

Several clubs, including my own club, Salford, had been holding private meetings to consider a possible breakaway. I immediately realised that the coaching committee's report, however superficial, needed to be completed as a matter of urgency. The report addressed twenty issues and began as follows:

> Rugby League must continue to adapt to changing circumstances so that its future as a major sport is assured. The fact that Rugby League has two governing bodies, however, is a significant constraint to a coherent development policy. Unless the structure of our game is reviewed to assess its capacity to adapt in the face of uncertain and unpredictable social trends, it may lose the energy and will to survive in its present form.
>
> Responding to crises as they arrive is not a development policy, and although there is a great deal to be optimistic about, a confident and bold strategy is essential. There needs to be investment in time, ideas, forward-planning and funding. The temptation to redistribute funds to member clubs may be understandable in the current climate as survival is uppermost in their thinking along with ground improvements, team strengthening, marketing and cash flow. The Rugby Football League council, however, has a responsibility to govern and to manage its funds to take into account the overall good of the game but it must also project a dynamic and thrustful organisation that reflects enterprise and initiative.

The report went on to make the following recommendations:

General
   1 That this Report be considered by the management board and
     council with a view to taking immediate and positive action.

Administration
   2 That the role and structure of the Rugby Football League
     council be examined to see if it has the flexibility and capacity
     to respond to the need for reform.
   3 That the present voting system be modified to introduce
     differential voting for first- and second-division clubs.

Finance
   4 That the current policy on the equal redistribution of central
     funds be reformed.

5 That the levy system in its present form be abandoned and replaced with an alternative.

6 That the allocation of sponsorship and TV payments to clubs be significantly revised.

Promotion And Marketing

7 That a more expansive and ambitious marketing and promotional strategy be initiated.

League Structure

8 That existing competitions be examined to see if a reduction of the number of overall fixtures is desirable or practical.

9 That the role of the colts league be examined to assess its future role and cost-effectiveness.

Development

10 That we increase our investment in development from the current level of 4 per cent.

11 That a network of development officers with clearly defined roles be established in conjunction with BARLA.

Coaching

12 That we continue to support and expand the National Coaching Scheme.

13 That clubs put greater emphasis on improving the professionalism of their coaches.

14 That we obtain sponsorship for the National Coaching Scheme.

15 That we invest in the production of first-class coaching materials.

16 That we continue to invest in the preparation of international teams.

BARLA

17 That links with BARLA are strengthened.

18 That we resolve our conflict with BARLA over colts and youth rugby.

Schools

19 That the English Schools RL be invited to contribute to an overall development strategy.

Referees

20 That the Referees Society be invited to draw up a referees' development policy.

I completed the report in time to get it to council on the day the breakaway clubs were intending to force the issue. I spoke to a tense David Oxley and a shocked Joe Seddon of St Helens, the Rugby Football League chairman, prior to going into the meeting. Joe was very angry because his own club chairman had attended the breakaway meetings but had not kept him informed of events. He felt that as chairman of the RFL he had been placed in an untenable position.

I went into council determined to oppose the breakaway, but to support moves for major reform along the lines laid down in the report. For the recommendations to stand a chance of realisation, the vote on the breakaway needed to be delayed until frank discussion had taken place. Along with Leigh's representative, another member of the breakaway group, I voted with the main body of council in favour of discussion taking place; this was in fact carried as the breakaway clubs failed to get a two-thirds majority. When I later explained to the Salford chairman, John Wilkinson, why I had not gone along with the initial vote I assured him that I was voting for discussion in the first place so that everyone could make up their minds on the issues. Simply to come to council with a mandate to vote without discussion was not the way things should be done. John accepted my explanation, but I was angry that Maurice Lindsay of Wigan had suggested to him that I was not representing Salford's best interests. I later challenged Maurice on this particular point, but he felt that I should have shown solidarity or, as he put it, 'steel' in the face of some of the unambitious second-division clubs.

As discussion took place common sense began to prevail. Various concessions were made over a reduction in the levy and a redistribution of funds in favour of more successful clubs. Maurice Lindsay and Roy Waudby recognised the efforts that were being made by the Rugby Football League to meet the very valid criticisms of the leading clubs and moved that if the council was prepared to sanction the changes proposed in our report and to take a critical look at the whole structure of the game then they were happy to work within the existing by-laws.

I am not sure how many council members present that day fully understood how close to the brink we were. Joe Seddon's skills as chairman and David Oxley's wisdom and statesmanship were critical factors in the preservation of the status quo. Certainly the council, for all its faults as a monolith, showed just enough flexibility to ride out the storm, whilst maintaining the restraining influence which is essential in the process of evolution if cataclysmic events such as the original breakaway in 1895 are to remain rare events.

It is true that the timely arrival at council of the coaching committee's development strategy played a significant part in events because Joe Seddon was able to point to it as evidence of goodwill on the part of the Rugby Football League. Without that document the credibility of the management board might have been severely tested. The coaching committee was disbanded in 1988, most of its recommendations have now been set in place and the report gathers dust on some forgotten shelf. Rapid changes in personnel on the council mean that, for many, its existence is unknown.

But if there had been no report, if sensible people had not urged caution, if either council or the leading breakaway activists had been totally inflexible, then events might have taken a totally different course.

My relief that the breakaway had been averted was partly influenced by my fear that, with the visit of the 1986 Kangaroos now on the horizon, any upheaval would jeopardise our chances. Following the Kiwi series we were naturally confident that we had come up with a successful formula and had no reason to doubt that we would beat France convincingly in the build-up to the Australian Tests in the autumn. The French, however, have always been unpredictable, and on their own soil they play with pride and what the press like to call Gallic flair – in other words, they throw the ball about.

Preparations for the visit to Avignon in February 1986 were affected by Arctic conditions in the north of England and our final session had been restricted to a sports hall. Avignon, a delightful medieval walled city, was enjoying an early spring, so we quickly took advantage of the sunshine and got down to the business of preparing for a Test match which counted

Wigan back-rower Ian Potter was an important element in Maurice Bamford's Great Britain selections, not least for his tireless defensive displays and solid grafting.

for points in the qualifying stages for the 1988 World Cup final. At this stage, we had collected one point from the drawn third Test against New Zealand.

We made only two changes from the Kiwi Tests, bringing in Henderson Gill and Shaun Wane for Lydon and Goodway, but you would not have thought it was the same team. Although David Watkinson monopolised the scrums, the midfield failed to stamp any authority on the match, and it took a genuine stroke of fortune to give Great Britain a 10–2 half-time lead. Shaun Wane, breaking from midfield, threw a speculative and obviously forward inside pass which brushed a Frenchman's arm, so playing Hanley onside; the centre had an easy stroll to the posts. Although Schofield had a try disallowed after the restart, it was the French back three who dominated the play, only to be undone time and again by the poverty of the threequarters' finishing. It took a magical piece of initiative by their scrum-half-turned-full-back, Gilles Dumas, to put France back in the running and, in the drama of the final quarter, it was he who converted a penalty to lock the scores at 10–10.

France: Dumas; Couston, Fourquet, Maury, Laroche; Espugna, Entat; Chantal, Baco, Titeux, Guy Laforgue, Palanque, Bernabé
Substitutes: Rabot for Titeux after 36 minutes, Bergé for Laroche after 77 minutes
Scorers: try – Dumas; goals – Dumas (3)

Great Britain: Burke (Widnes); Drummond (Leigh), Schofield (Hull), Hanley (Wigan), Gill (Wigan); Tony Myler (Widnes), Fox (Featherstone Rovers); Crooks (Hull), Watkinson (Hull KR), Wane (Wigan), Potter (Wigan), Fieldhouse (Widnes), Pinner (St Helens)
Substitutes: Edwards (Wigan) and James (Halifax) not used
Scorers: try – Hanley; goals – Crooks (3)

Referee: K. Roberts (Australia)

Some of the leading players blamed our poor showing on our preparation and on the comparatively low bonus they received for French matches which, they thought, reflected an out-of-date attitude by the Rugby Football League. For the return match in Wigan on 1 March we introduced new caps in Tony Marchant, David Laws, Kevin Rayne and Neil James, if only because of injuries to Pinner, Burke, Grayshon and Hanley. David Watkinson was made captain for the first time.

The result, a 24–10 victory, may not have seemed entirely convincing, but it reflected credit on the team's reaction to the disappointments of Avignon. Second-rowers James and Rayne seized their opportunity avidly, providing the firepower, strength and mobility that Great Britain had lacked. Schofield was back to his brilliant best, scoring one of his side's clinically executed tries and laying on a début try for Marchant. The French struggled to come to terms with the bitterly cold weather and the hard pitch at Central Park, but with Couston adding two tries to his hat-trick of the previous year and Palanque posing a constant threat out wide, they still provided a formidable obstacle for the growing Great Britain team.

Great Britain: Lydon (Wigan); Drummond (Leigh), Schofield (Hull), Marchant (Castleford), Laws (Hull KR); Tony Myler (Widnes), Fox (Featherstone Rovers); Crooks (Hull), Watkinson (Hull KR), Fieldhouse (Widnes), Kevin Rayne (Leeds), James (Halifax), Potter (Wigan)
Substitutes: Platt (St Helens) for Fieldhouse after 73 minutes; Edwards (Wigan) not used
Scorers: tries – Drummond, Schofield, James, Marchant; goals – Crooks (2), Schofield (2)

France: Dumas; Couston, Bergé, Fourquet, Laroche; Espugna, Entat; Chantal, Baco, Titeux, Guy Laforgue, Palanque, Bernabé
Substitutes: Rabot for Chantal after 66 minutes, Pallarès for Espugna after 70 minutes
Scorers: tries – Couston (2); goal – Dumas

Referee: K. Roberts (Australia)

Maurice, Phil and myself admitted that we still had a lot of hard work to put in, and we named a thirty-man squad to report for summer training at Carnegie College, Leeds, where we hoped fitness levels would be raised. The squad was invited to a special launch at Shaw Hill where Maurice outlined his plans to the players and invited them to sign a pledge. Each player was handed a training manual specially produced to mark the beginning of our campaign against Australia which also contained a statement requiring each player to commit himself to a summer of hard physical training. We felt that by appealing to each player individually they would be more likely to make the necessary sacrifices to achieve a higher level of fitness.

During July Maurice and I travelled to Sydney and Brisbane to check on the trans-Tasman Test matches, to reconnoitre potential hotels and training facilities for the 1988 tour and to observe Australian club football at first hand. On the plane an English supporter recognised Maurice and came over to introduce himself. He also thought he knew me and wondered why Maurice roared with laughter when I denied that I was Dick Gemmell, the former Great Britain manager. I was later to get my own back on Maurice when we visited the Rushcutter's Bay Hotel to assess its suitability as accommodation for the Great Britain team. I howled with delight at Maurice's mortification when the receptionist said, 'Don't I know you – aren't you Alex Murphy?' Maurice looked at me and said, 'Touché, mate.'

Injury to Harry Pinner meant that David Watkinson assumed the Great Britain captaincy against France in 1986 and retained it for the visit of the Kangaroos later in the year. Never the prettiest of hookers, Watkinson was another Bamford favourite for his hard work around the ruck.

I was ready for bed at 7:30 the morning we arrived, but Maurice told me that if I was to cope with jet-lag then I must retire at the normal time. Showered and breakfasted we went round to present our credentials at the New South Wales Rugby League HQ. I couldn't help comparing our own modest HQ situated in the Leeds suburb of Chapeltown with this impressive location in the centre of Sydney.

Rugby League in Sydney is big business. Every day newspapers fill three pages with Rugby League news, information, and match reports. The modest coverage we get in English papers suffers badly by comparison. I was beginning to understand why the game enjoys such a high profile as I examined the colourful and glossy *Rugby League Week*, an attractive magazine-type newspaper for Rugby League enthusiasts. Since 1986 I have to say our own *Rugby Leaguer* and *Open Rugby* have moved upmarket and reflect great credit on the editors. During our stay in Sydney we were also able to watch Rugby League on TV at several points throughout the week and see the game's top players featuring regularly in advertisements. I knew that we in Britain still had a long way to go to attract this quality of media attention and sponsorship.

Maurice and I visited several Australian clubs and observed training sessions taking place in pleasant conditions. Although it was winter the day-time temperature still touched 70°; I contrasted this with cold, wet, wintry evenings at Castleford or Widnes. Australian players certainly have a superior training environment, but I also recognised that their level of professionalism was way ahead of the majority of British clubs. Their players were expected to arrive at pre-season training ready to be tested for strength, speed and endurance. This meant that they had to carry out training schedules in their own time, whereas British players tended to arrive at pre-season training in order to get fit.

Talking to the famous coach Jack Gibson and his assistant Ron Massey, I realised the debt Australian Rugby League owes to American grid-iron football, in terms of training methods, philosophy and strategy. Gibson talks about 'offence' and 'defence'. He reduces the game to a basic and simple strategy: if the opposition don't have the ball, then they don't score. Off-the-cuff rugby is not acceptable to Australian coaches; they require their players to stick rigidly to the game plan. In one sense Australian rugby could be regarded as predictable and repetitive with little scope for flair. I don't see it like that, however, because their players demonstrate such great technical efficiency in passing, tackling and support play. Maurice and I came away from our talk with Gibson convinced that his simple ideas about 'winning rugby' made sense and that we could adapt some of them to our needs. Later on we had a further meeting with Ron Massey, one of the shrewdest football analysts in the business who used video analysis as an integral part of team preparation. In 1986 not all British coaches used video analysis other than sitting their players in front of unedited chunks of tape without any real purpose or structure.

Our visit to the new Parramatta Stadium provided a vivid contrast with many of our own decaying Edwardian grounds. This stadium, financed by the local council, had identical stands running the full length of both sides of the pitch. Behind the posts on a grassy mound families gathered and picnicked in the warm sunshine as they watched the reserves play before the big match. The scene was colourful and I observed that a whole cross-section of Australian society attend and watch Rugby League just as they do cricket in England. The game appeals as much to professional people as to other sectors of society, although, as in Great Britain, there was a pleasing absence of gangs of chanting youths tanked up on alcohol. As Maurice and I enjoyed a privileged view from the NSWRL hospitality box we both agreed that this was a view of Rugby League in the next century, and we were envious.

While I was at Parramatta I visited the home dressing-room to present Brett Kenny with a replica of the Lance Todd Trophy which he had been awarded as the outstanding player of that magnificent Challenge Cup final between Wigan and Hull in 1985. The Salford Red Devils Association are custodians of the trophy awarded in memory of Lance Todd, the New Zealander who successfully coached the pre-war Salford team. Brett had not been able to attend the original award ceremony which took place a few days after the final as he had returned home to Australia. I'm sure that he will cherish the memory of playing in a winning team at the famous stadium and collecting the Lance Todd Trophy, particularly in a match that has gone down in history as perhaps the greatest Cup final ever seen.

Shaun Edwards's potential was recognised by Maurice Bamford at a very early stage, and he became a part of Great Britain's plans from 1985 onwards, although his versatility confined him to the bench for most of 1986.

Several Great Britain Test players were over in Sydney at the time, fulfilling short-term contracts with Balmain and Norths. Tony Myler, Lee Crooks, Garry Schofield, Deryck Fox and Des Drummond joined us for lunch one day so that we could get some first-hand observations on the type of rugby they were experiencing. All of them emphasised the professionalism of the Australian game, but they all agreed that Australian players were not supermen and bled like the rest of us. Maurice and I enjoyed meeting the players and we were reassured by their optimism. They looked fit and well and were all giving a good account of themselves on the field.

During my stay in Sydney, I negotiated on behalf of Salford with an outstanding young forward called Geoff Selby of the St George club. Geoff was on the fringe of Test honours and wanted to visit England to gain experience. He had all the qualities of a modern player with a fine physique and an explosive burst of speed. He was to become very popular with the Salford spectators who were as shocked as I was to hear of his tragic death in a car crash in 1988.

A great part of Australia's success lies in its production line of young players and when Maurice and I visited a school to see this at first hand we came away greatly impressed. Inter-house matches were taking place within the various year groups, all of which were keenly contested; at a glance I could see potential professional players. We joined the boys at the end of the day for a barbecue and their enthusiasm for Rugby League was obvious. Great efforts are being made to establish Rugby League as a major game in the comprehensive schools of Britain, but we still have some way to catch up, and we, of course, have to compete with soccer and Rugby Union.

Interest in the first Test match between Australia and New Zealand was building up in the city and a good crowd was expected at the Sydney Cricket Ground. Maurice and I got there early on the day of the match and walked around the famous ground in warm sunshine, soaking up the atmosphere. A new stadium was being erected close by, and the cricket ground's days as a venue for Rugby League were numbered. Tradition and nostalgia are important parts of the culture of any sport, but sport has a duty to invest in its future; Australia was doing that.

Australia won the match fairly easily although there was a spot mid-way through the match when the Kiwis looked dangerous. Defences were always on top and open rugby was at a premium. This was the Australian system of pressure rugby: getting over the gain-line, kicking effectively and supporting the ball-carrier. It was in evidence again in the second Test at Lang Park in Brisbane. The Australian Test machine was awesome and the midfield trio of Sterling, Lewis and Pearce was magnificent. All three were at the peak of their careers and dictated tactics. Peter Sterling's non-stop play at scrum-half, spraying out passes, switching the line of attack and putting in precision line-kicks, confirmed him as the world's best. Wally Lewis dominated the match with his powerful surges and amazing ability to offload in the tightest of situations. This magical pair was brilliantly supported by the running and tackling of Wayne Pearce, the archetypal modern loose forward. When you add to these such players as Gene Miles, Mal Meninga, Michael O'Connor and Garry Jack, you are talking about a better-than-average team.

The Kiwis played well, which gave us some consolation. But as we sat there looking for weaknesses in the Australian line-up we were both silent, perhaps afraid to say what we were thinking. We certainly didn't attempt to delude ourselves as to the magnitude of the task ahead. We had had a relatively short period to rebuild our Test side, and although we had made great progress in terms of fitness, attitude, commitment and team-work, we wondered whether it was sufficient.

4

Return of the 'Roos

Before taking the squad to Lilleshall in preparation for the visit of the 1986 Australians we arranged to play three trial matches. The most important of these was to be Probables versus Possibles at Central Park prior to the season starting. In the event it did more harm than good, with the Probables sneaking home by a narrow margin of 2 points with over 60 points being scored in total. Hardly convincing in view of our supposed emphasis on defence!

We delayed the visit to Lilleshall until the first week of September because several leading players were not expected back from spells in Australia until late August. Even then, a number were not able to undertake the rigorous programme that had been prepared because they had picked up injuries in pre-season warm-up matches. There is nothing worse in arranging international training sessions than to have players queuing up for treatment and unable to join in. One of the reasons we had moved to one extended get-together at Lilleshall, instead of the midweek evening sessions which had been the traditional way teams were prepared in the past, was this very problem.

One of the areas of team preparation we were keen to explore was that of sports psychology. Were there things that we did which were counter-productive or conversely, were there things we could do which would enhance player performance? To help us in our deliberations we enlisted the help of Alma Thomas, principal of Bedford College of Physical Education. As a sports psychologist she had carried out work with British athletes and had some knowledge of British Rugby Union preparation. Phil Larder had heard her address a Sports Council conference and believed that her ideas could have relevance to our work.

Alma was shrewd enough to know that being paraded in front of the Great Britain team to 'do psychology' at them was not the way to approach the subject. On the other hand, she was more than prepared to share ideas with us to see if we could make use of them. In particular she believed we should work on our own communication skills. We were certainly reassured to know that our move from a 'telling' mode to one where we expected players to express themselves and take responsibility for decision-making was one she approved of. The idea that players constantly need to be told things before they can play is, of course, nonsense. At the highest level you need players not only confident in their own ability and that of their team-mates, but also able to think for themselves.

We recognised that our players lagged a long way behind Australian players in self-esteem, simply because the Australians had got into the habit of winning whereas we had got into a habit of losing. One of Alma's key suggestions to counter this was individual and team goal-setting, getting players to target certain goals so that communication between coach and players should become more productive. She suggested that each player should fill in a simple worksheet and that this could then be used as a basis for discussion. I'm not sure that we achieved a great deal in this area, because making a behavioural change in anyone with a lifetime of attitudes and habits already in place is pretty challenging. Nevertheless, Maurice and Phil used the worksheets at Lilleshall and the players gave full co-operation. The answers were confidential, but if I reveal that Lee Crooks's ambition was to captain Great Britain in a victory over Australia you can get a flavour of the responses.

Another area we explored was that of motivation. Different players respond to different stimuli, and a blanket approach to motivation could be counter-productive. Anxiety can also cause players to perform below par. One way to reduce it is to practice mental rehearsal during moments of relaxation – putting it simply, to visualise yourself carrying out skills successfully, such as catching a high ball under pressure. We were prepared to explore every avenue to ensure that when our players went out against Australia they would be confident and not handicapped by anxiety or self-doubt.

Away from psychology, the coaches were also keen to improve the Great Britain kicking game. To assist with this Dave Aldred, a teacher from Bristol who had had a successful spell as a kicker in American Football, joined us to run a kicking clinic. Dave had been used during the 1985 Kiwi series, and his influence on some of our kickers was obvious. He has a phenomenal ability to kick a rugby ball high and long, and he passed on specific techniques which benefitted our key kickers, Joe Lydon in particular.

The week went well and the players ran through all their training drills with steely determination. Lilleshall had worked for them in preparation for the Kiwis, and they genuinely believed that it would work for them against the Australians. Attitude and commitment were words that echoed round the training field, and any player lacking in enthusiasm got the rough edge of Maurice's tongue. Team spirit was excellent, and I was confident that we would give the Australians a shock.

The Australian touring party arrived in the north of England to great media interest and public anticipation. Wally Lewis captained a team which included the familiar names of Peter Sterling, Mal Meninga, Gene Miles, and Brett Kenny, but overall it was the youngest ever touring party. A crowd of 30,000 turned up at Central Park for the opening tour match against Wigan and the Kangaroos began in convincing style to take a 20–2 lead after forty-seven minutes, before Wigan fought back to a final score of 26–18. It seemed that Australia were vulnerable; if Wigan could score three tries against them then surely Great Britain were capable of the same? In the next three matches, however, Australia were to amass 130 points at an average of 42 points a match.

In selecting our own Test squad we relied heavily on players who had served us well against the Kiwis. We were confident that we knew our best combination and that we had players as skilful as Australia's. Our view was that, if we were to take the game to Australia, we needed a full-back who could not only run the ball out but could also kick well. Despite Joe Lydon's hesitant performance for Lancashire in the Roses match, we selected him ahead of more established full-backs such as Mick Burke, George Fairbairn and Keith Mumby.

The wing positions were not so clear-cut as Des Drummond was out with injury. Henderson Gill was the obvious choice for the left wing, while Tony Marchant, who had been selected at centre against France, had had a successful Cup final appearance with Castleford, and during the summer

Wigan's exuberant and unorthodox winger Henderson Gill leaves Wally Lewis (left) and Terry Lamb in his wake as he breaks during the first Test against Australia in 1986. Gill was a constant thorn in the Kangaroos' side, both in this series and down under in 1988.

had played in Brisbane alongside Wally Lewis. Because of our emphasis on defence we decided to select Tony for the right wing.

The centres selected themselves – Schofield and Hanley, surely as good a combination as any in the world. Tony Myler was the obvious choice at stand-off; his summer experience for Balmain in Sydney was ideal preparation for facing Wally Lewis. There was a strong lobby for the recall of Andy Gregory as scrum-half, but because Deryek Fox was the man in possession and had given an impeccable performance for Yorkshire against Lancashire, his superior tackle rate won the day.

Kevin Ward and John Fieldhouse were selected as props, Kevin replacing the hero of the Kiwi series, Jeff Grayshon, who was now pushing 37. David Watkinson was the hooker and team captain. David had been successful against the Kiwis, and it was felt that his aggressive, no-nonsense style was essential. Although Lee Crooks was better suited to prop, his ball-handling skills gave him one of the second-row positions, while the other went to Ian Potter, whose defensive qualities were a must. Andy Goodway took the loose forward position because Harry Pinner had had a series of injuries and was not considered.

We met at Shaw Hill on the Monday before the first Test. To counter the threat of boredom we had devised a week of activities using different venues – one session at Blackpool, another at Lancaster University, from where we called in at Barrow to see Cumbria play Australia. We visited Old Trafford and used other club training facilities, and by varying the programme we hoped to keep the players fresh and alert. In the early part of the week players were free to relax in the evenings and enjoy a couple of beers as they chatted and played snooker or cards. Most players reverted to soft drinks by the end of the week, but if Kevin Ward believes that a glass of Guinness helps him to sleep, who were we to disagree? We were, after all, in the business of getting the best out of our players.

One of our concerns as the week progressed was Ellery Hanley's fitness. Ellery had hurt his knee playing for Wigan against St Helens and was not able to run without some pain. The dilemma was whether Ellery on one leg was better than no Ellery. After discussions with the doctor, physio and Ellery himself the consensus was that, with treatment, he would be fit to play on Saturday.

After the final training session on the Friday the countdown for the Test match began. Following the evening meal the players met for the final in-depth meeting. First, Maurice talked passionately about pride, and spoke of other heroic moments in history when Britain were underdogs. He quoted Nelson's speech at Trafalgar and Churchill's Battle of Britain clarion call about 'the few'. He said that in the future people would be able to recognise the players in that room as the heroes who had beaten Australia and turned the tide of Rugby League supremacy.

Next he repeated the game plan, which was based on closing down the options of Lewis and Sterling, using close man-for-man marking and kicking the ball deep into the Australian half whenever possible. It had been decided not to drive the ball in close to the play-the-ball, but to play a slightly wider attacking game. We were not sure that meeting the Australian pack head-on was to our advantage.

Phil Larder provided a detailed breakdown of each Australian player and their particular characteristics, using edited sections of video to illustrate normal Australian patterns of play. He emphasised control and discipline, particularly the virtues of keeping it simple. Finally I presented each player with his Great Britain shirt for him to keep in his possession until the match. We felt that this ritual could help their psychological preparation, almost as if they were knights receiving their shields before battle.

We woke on the morning of the match to lashing rain and gale-force winds. Although it would be the same for both sides it was not what we wanted. The players were free to get up when they liked, but they had specially ordered pre-match meals at set times. Each player was scheduled to meet with the coaches for a ten-minute motivational chat. Maurice set great store by these chats, to gauge how each player was feeling and to reassure them if they were unduly nervous.

After a morning that seemed to last for ever we climbed on to the coach and set off for Old Trafford. The dressing-room soon became a hive of activity as the players set about their individual preparation for the match, each one following long-practised rituals of warming up, getting strapping for old war wounds, putting on each article of clothing and equipment in preferred order. The kit man, doctor and physio buzzed around seeing to every whim, while the coaches moved from player to player to remind them of their particular duties. Some players were ready early and sat with concentration on their faces; others were still padding about in bare feet.

Finally the moment had come. There was nothing left to do but for Maurice to wish the players well, and for us to shake hands and express our confidence. There was a bang on the door, the referee blew his whistle and I led the team along the corridor, down the tunnel and on to the pitch, into an overwhelming wall of noise from 50,000 supporters who believed that today we would make history. Once the pre-match ceremonies were over, Maurice, Phil and I made our way to the bench along with the substitutes. I was more nervous that I could ever remember.

With a strong following wind and heavy rain it was vital that Great Britain should repeatedly pump the ball deep into Australian territory, but from the outset they seemed reluctant to do this. In the opening exchanges they even moved the ball across the pitch in front of their own posts, enabling Henderson Gill to scurry away on an overlap. This early breakout brought a roar of approval from the crowd, but the insistence on moving the ball flat across the pitch, when handling was difficult in the wet conditions, meant that ground and possession invariably were lost.

The first Australian try was relatively simple. After nine minutes Gene Miles roared through a wide gap to score unopposed, when Hanley had allowed himself to be pulled in to tackle Brett Kenny, who was already lined up by Tony Myler. When Michael O'Connor scored twice after twenty-one and thirty-two minutes, the fault again lay with Great Britain's threequarters and their man-for-man marking, both centres finding themselves stranded in no-man's land, unable to make a telling tackle. At half-time we were staring right down the barrel.

The second half threatened to tell a different story when, following a good build-up, Lee Crooks found sufficient space to release a superb pass to Garry Schofield who raced in for a try close to the posts. Four minutes later Great Britain moved the ball swiftly across their own 22, Goodway handed on to Myler who floated out a perfect pass to create the overlap for Joe Lydon, who swept on to it at full pace. He sprinted away clear of the cover and outpaced the Australian full-back, Garry Jack, to score a brilliant try in the corner. Great Britain were back in the game.

Joe Lydon sets off for the spectacular eighty-metre try which brought Great Britain back into running in the first Kangaroo Test of 1986. Selected at full-back for his kicking game, Lydon was always more dangerous to the Australians on the run.

It was only two minutes later, however, following a misfield from the kick-off, that Lewis was able to burst through a weak double tackle to put the giant Miles between the posts. Great Britain's resistance collapsed, and there followed a succession of tries from O'Connor, Miles and Jack to push Australia's total to 38 points. A late try from Garry Schofield gave Great Britain a final tally of 16 points, but little compensation.

Great Britain: Lydon (Wigan); Marchant (Castleford), Schofield (Hull), Hanley (Wigan), Gill (Wigan); Tony Myler (Widnes), Fox (Featherstone Rovers); Ward (Castleford), Watkinson (Hull KR), Fieldhouse (Widnes), Crooks (Hull), Potter (Wigan), Goodway (Wigan)
Substitutes: Edwards (Wigan) and Platt (St Helens) not used
Scorers: tries – Schofield (2), Lydon; goals – Crooks, Gill

Australia: Jack; Kiss, Kenny, Miles, O'Connor; Lewis, Sterling; Dowling, Simmons, Roach, Cleal, Niebling, Lindner
Substitutes: Meninga for Kiss after 55 minutes, Lamb for Lindner after 77 minutes
Scorers: tries – Miles (3), O'Connor (3), Jack; goals – O'Connor (5)

Referee: J. Rascagnères (France)

A losers' dressing-room is like nowhere else. Despair, anger, frustration, grief, pain – all the emotions are there exposed for all to see. No one looks anyone in the eye in case they see blame. Some players head for the bath within seconds, others sit slumped, staring at the floor. The doctor and physio move round administering comfort and treatment. The coaches have little to say because it has all been said. Old Trafford on 25 October 1986 at 4:30 p.m. was all of this and more. Eighteen months of preparation, and all our hopes and aspirations, had been blown away in eighty minutes. At that precise moment our depression was unbearable.

Maurice and I moved to face the press, who stood huddled together in a confined space, almost as dejected and crestfallen as we were. They too had shared the impossible dream, only it had turned out to be a nightmare. We did not try to make excuses, but I was as surprised as they were when Maurice announced, 'I will name an unchanged side for the second Test. I have faith in my players and I believe that they can do better.' As we left the press room Maurice apologised to me for not telling me of his decision beforehand. 'I saw the depression in the dressing-room,' he said, 'and I needed to give the players a lift.' This was a marvellous, spontaneous gesture, but it removed the opportunity for any minor changes which could have commended themselves after a period of reflection.

Next day I rang Maurice and Phil because I knew that someone had to begin the process of repairing morale. I knew exactly how they were both feeling because I'd shared it with them, but I knew Maurice in particular would be taking the defeat very hard and that press and radio accounts would be adding to his mental anguish. At the end of our conversation I sensed that Maurice was in a better frame of mind as his good humour began to re-emerge. I felt better for talking to him and we agreed to meet within days to begin the post mortem.

Maurice, Phil and myself all repeatedly studied the match video and made detailed notes. Phil, in particular, was able to provide extensive statistical information, and of all the facts and figures he provided the most telling was the territorial graph. This presented in stark terms the amount of time we had spent in the Australian defensive quarter of the pitch and the amount of time we had spent in our own defensive quarter. In the whole match we were only in a strong attacking position for eight minutes whereas Australia spent well over twenty minutes in our defensive area.

We examined the high error count of dropped passes and missed tackles and tried to pinpoint the reason. Was there something we had missed? There was no doubt that Sterling and Lewis as a combination were majestic. Their ability to control the game was a telling factor, their clever switches of play and precision passing a constant threat. But a nagging doubt forced itself into my thoughts, that our players were psychologically incapable of winning. Were they so in awe of Australia that it caused them to freeze in situations of stress or pressure? Before we went into camp for the second Test at Elland Road we were forced to make one change. Ellery Hanley was admitted to hospital for a knee operation which confirmed that he hadn't been fit for the first Test. Ellery had passed our physical tests to prove his fitness because he is such a great competitor and perfectionist.

Despite playing in a beaten team, Garry Schofield cemented his reputation as a try-sniffer by crossing the Kangaroos line five times in 1986. Here he beats Bryan Niebling's despairing dive to touch down in the first Test at Old Trafford.

However, he had not displayed his usual confidence, probably worried that he might break down, and on this occasion our gamble had not paid off. Barry Ledger was brought in on the right wing and Tony Marchant was moved to left centre in Ellery's stead.

We moved into Shaw Hill on the Wednesday and confined ourselves to training at club grounds close by, although we did travel for one session at Elland Road. Maurice had recovered his enthusiasm, although he was a little aggressive with one or two unfortunate members of the press who he felt had been a little too personal with their criticism. Once again, preparation seemed to go well, and the players pledged their determination not to be humiliated again.

The Elland Road ground in Leeds was packed to the gills with 30,000 spectators on Saturday 8 November, and for the first twenty-eight minutes of the match Great Britain's defence and general play lived up to the crowd's expectations. The moment of truth came when Barry Ledger, fielding the ball deep in his own half, began a lateral run to set up an attack which found Tony Myler striding majestically towards the Australian line with plenty of support. As he approached the exposed Garry Jack, Myler inexplicably opted to kick ahead rather than pass to the unmarked Garry Schofield, and a certain try went begging. Great Britain were never to threaten Australia seriously again. Slowly but surely, despite periodic bouts of bright play, the mistakes began to creep in, and by the end of the match the handling error count of eighteen exceeded the first Test total of fourteen.

Following a moment of defensive indecision, the giant Australian second row, Noel Cleal, stepped through two tackles to gallop for the line before offloading to Bob Lindner, up in support like the man he had replaced on the tour, the injured Wayne Pearce, to claim the try. Five minutes later, Michael O'Connor got free on the left flank, easily outpacing the cover. Joe Lydon was on hand to tackle, but O'Connor kicked ahead and Lydon hesitated, probably reminded of the ten minutes he had spent in the sin bin at Old Trafford for a late tackle. Although his tackle would have been punished for obstruction, it would perhaps have been a legitimate decision for him to have taken instead of pulling out of the tackle and allowing O'Connor to score.

The second half was a nightmare for Great Britain, with the crowd chanting 'what a load of rubbish' at our lowest point. The pack continued to work hard with Ward, Goodway and Potter to the fore, but with Crooks losing the ball on seven occasions, they seemed to have a death wish. One particular try epitomised that. After Great Britain had won the ball from a scrum, Lewis was able to rip the ball away from a stand-up tackle on Myler and spin a pass out to the right, which freed Garry Jack to score in the corner. Down by 34–0, Great Britain had seen their lapses severely punished. Once again Garry Schofield scored a late try, but once again it was hardly a consolation.

Great Britain: Lydon (Wigan); Ledger (St Helens), Schofield (Hull), Marchant (Castleford), Gill (Wigan); Tony Myler (Widnes), Fox (Featherstone Rovers); Ward (Castleford), Watkinson (Hull KR), Fieldhouse (Widnes), Crooks (Hull), Potter (Wigan), Goodway (Wigan)
Substitutes: Edwards (Wigan) for Tony Myler after 58 minutes, Platt (St Helens) for Watkinson after 20 minutes
Scorer: try – Schofield

Australia: Jack; Shearer, Kenny, Miles, O'Connor; Lewis, Sterling; Dowling, Simmons, Dunn, Cleal, Niebling, Lindner
Substitutes: Lamb for Sterling after 78 minutes, Meninga for Niebling after 78 minutes
Scorers: tries – Jack (2), Lindner, Lewis, O'Connor, Kenny; goals – O'Connor (5)

Referee: J. Rascagnères (France)

Two days later Phil Larder and I met at Maurice's home to select the team for the final Test at Wigan. I was shocked and concerned at Maurice's appearance; he seemed to have aged dramatically and I knew he was taking responsibility for the defeats personally. I quickly set about the task of counselling him in an effort to reassure him that all was not lost and that I too shared the responsibility. We chatted as friends, and it was ideal therapy for both of us.

With personal confidence somewhat restored we started to examine the facts to see what we could build on. We knew that changes were necessary for tactical reasons and also to restore public confidence. It would mean that some players would have to be replaced, not necessarily those who had performed badly. Into this category came Deryck Fox. Despite being awarded Great Britain's man-of-the-match in the first Test and despite his incredibly high work rate, Deryck had not been incisive in midfield nor had he been able to get the attack moving. If we wanted to change our approach, we felt Andy Gregory would give us more variety, Deryck's superior defensive qualities apart.

We brought in a new left wing pairing of David Stephenson and John Basnett. Both were strong, experienced players and were exhibiting good club form. Changing the forwards was more problematic, but we decided with reluctance that John Fieldhouse, the hero of the Kiwi Tests, had not enjoyed the same success against Australia and that his prop position would be taken by Lee Crooks. Lee had had an awful second Test, but his ball-playing capabilities were essential. Ian Potter was replaced by Chris Burton, a forward who could run hard but had a tendency to tackle high. Andy Goodway was moved up to second row to allow Harry Pinner to take up his customary loose forward slot.

Tony Myler, confronted by Peter Sterling (left) and Gene Miles, puts out a desperate dive-pass to loose forward Andy Goodway in the first Test of 1986. Stand-off Myler will always be remembered for his brilliant break in the third Test at Wigan.

I was apprehensive about morale in camp as we prepared for the final encounter, but was pleasantly surprised by the players' attitude. They still had this illogical idea that they could beat Australia – if only!

I had discussed with the coaches changes to our normal preparation routine. They agreed with me that concentrating on 'unopposed team practice', with the players perfecting their understanding of the basic game plan, was the best approach. We also came up with the idea of running the team in the last two training sessions as if they were playing a match, with the coaches remaining on the touchline and the captain calling the shots. We decided to record errors in training as if it were the real thing. This change of emphasis went down well and meant that Maurice could observe from a distance and just call the team together every so often to reaffirm a few objectives. He had recovered his old vigour and sensed that the players were more confident that they had been previously.

We set off for Central Park, Wigan, on Saturday 22 November believing that we would do better. I had my doubts fifteen minutes before kick-off when Chris Burton approached me looking like Stan Laurel to say, 'I've left my Great Britain shirt in the wardrobe.' Suddenly our idea of presenting players with their shirts the night before a match seemed fairly stupid. I looked at Maurice and decided that he had enough on his plate. Coincidence is a funny thing, however, and when Phil Larder said that he happened to have a No. 12 shirt in his bag as a personal souvenir, I could hardly believe it. Burty got his shirt and Maurice never found out.

After only two minutes, following a tap penalty to Great Britain, a dropped ball and a missed high tackle by Burton, Gene Miles went over for a try. Great Britain rallied with Andy Gregory, Kevin Ward and Lee Crooks at the fore, but when Bob Lindner scooted over close to the posts after twenty-one minutes, everyone in the 20,000 crowd truly believed that another good hiding was on the way. Suddenly Harry Pinner threw out a superb pass to find Tony Myler totally wrong-footing Lewis and racing through the gap. In the second Test Myler had made a similar break and made the fatal decision to kick. This time, however, he spotted Schofield on his right, lobbed out an overhead pass and the centre avoided a despairing dive from O'Connor to score. It was half-time and the deficit was only 12–6.

Great Britain started the second half in confident style, running strongly, handling crisply and generally looking more capable. When the ball was moved across the pitch to the left Crooks, Myler and Stephenson handled before Schofield came on to an inside ball to score. Joe Lydon's conversion tied the scores at 12–12. However, Great Britain's physical and psychological advantage received a set-back when referee Rascagnères sent Burton to the sin bin for a high tackle, although Lewis's retaliation suggested that he should also have walked.

In the fifty-seventh minute Dale Shearer, Australia's right wing, broke away down the touchline and, as the cover approached, kicked ahead. John Basnett, who otherwise had an outstanding game, followed through and tackled him. Instead of awarding a penalty, the referee raced to the posts and signalled a penalty try. It was a decisive moment that perhaps turned the game. Although Great Britain forced their way back, with a goal and a drop-goal, to 15–18 with eleven minutes remaining, their hopes were finally dashed when Royce Simmons, the Australian hooker, ran from acting half-back on the sixth tackle and found Lewis in support. The Australian captain went on to mesmerise the defence as he scampered for the posts for a try that was never on – a mark of his true genius. After that Myler and Gill were both tackled close to the Australian line, but the Kangaroos held out to win the match 24–15 and to whitewash the series.

Great Britain: Lydon (Wigan); Gill (Wigan), Schofield (Hull), Stephenson (Wigan), Basnett (Widnes); Tony Myler (Widnes), Andy Gregory (Warrington); Ward (Castleford), Watkinson (Hull KR), Crooks (Hull), Burton (Hull KR), Goodway (Wigan), Pinner (St Helens)
Substitutes: Potter (Wigan) for Burton after 63 minutes; Edwards (Wigan) not used
Scorers: tries – Schofield (2); goals – Lydon (2), Gill; drop-goal – Schofield

Australian coach Don Furner visits a subdued Great Britain dressing-room to offer his condolencies to Maurice Bamford and Les Bettinson after the second Test at Leeds in 1986. A few short weeks later Bamford resigned from his position as national coach.

Australia: Jack; Shearer, Kenny, Miles, O'Connor; Lewis, Sterling; Dowling, Simmons, Dunn, Meninga, Niebling, Lindner
Substitutes: Lamb for Meninga after 78 minutes, Davidson for Dunn after 73 minutes
Scorers: tries – Miles, Lindner, Lewis, penalty; goals – O'Connor (4)

Referee: J. Rascagnères (France)

Maurice, Phil and I felt that something had been salvaged and the players had shown their capability; if only they had displayed this form earlier. Every player had distinguished himself, none more so than Andy Gregory who had been at the heart of everything. Kevin Ward had enjoyed a magnificent series, while Lee Crooks had at last come good in both attack and defence. Above all, I was pleased for Maurice who had finally had his efforts partially rewarded. It would have been a travesty of justice if he had come away from the series without a glimmer of hope or a sign of progress.

5

From Maurice to Mal

After the Test series I needed to get back to normality. It seemed that for months every waking hour had been taken up with the demands of international rugby, and now I needed to concentrate on my family and my job. Being Great Britain manager is a rare privilege but it is an honorary position with no salary. I planned to take things easy for a couple of months as there were no pressing international engagements.

I had mixed feelings over whether I wanted to continue as Great Britain manager. Part of me wondered whether I needed all the pressure that the job created. But when I received a 'phone call from Maurice Bamford late · one evening in December 1986 to tell me that he had just tendered his resignation as Great Britain coach, I was absolutely stunned.

Maurice went on to explain that concern for his wife, Rita, who did not enjoy good health, had forced him to consider his future. He felt that being away for ten weeks on the 1988 tour would be too much and his first priority was his wife. Although for Maurice the tour was the peak of his ambition, his family loyalty far exceeded his commitment to Rugby League. There was little I could say because the decision had been made. I thanked him for all he had achieved and for his friendship. He emphasised that I should continue as manager, but it seemed that my enthusiasm had been dented by his resignation, and perhaps my time was up.

Maurice Bamford's contribution to our international revival was much greater than the record shows. He was there at the beginning when much had to be done to regain the confidence of players and public alike. Maurice's personality, particularly his patriotic pride, was infectious. It communicated itself to his players and to the fans on the terraces. He was, after all, a man of the people who had devoted his life to Rugby League and, despite many a set-back, had got to the top.

Working with Phil Larder and me, he set about bringing organisation and credibility to the Great Britain set-up. Procedures for selection and team preparation became established and continuity was encouraged. Most of the players he used in 1985 and 1986 became permanent fixtures in the Great Britain team and all of them benefitted from a more professional approach. His legacy was a strong squad of players and a clear sense of direction.

When I was called to Rugby Football League HQ to meet the management board I was pleased to find that they wanted me to continue as manager and they sought my views on a replacement coach. I suggested that there were several possibilities, but that holding a formal series of interviews would not be appropriate as the board had already conducted interviews for the previous appointment and there were no new candidates. After much discussion the board said they would convene a meeting in January 1987 and they would like me to return with a firm recommendation for their approval.

As I drove away I reflected on the coaches who could fill the criteria of an outstanding coaching background; public credibility; acceptability to the board; adaptability to the existing system; and proven Australian experience. Several coaches filled some of the criteria but only two filled all of them – Mal Reilly of Castleford and Roger Millward of Hull KR.

Mal had been a tearaway loose forward with Castleford in the late 1960s before touring Australia in 1970 with the last successful Lions team. He eventually returned there to enjoy an outstanding period with Manly, appearing in two Grand Finals, before returning to England in 1974 to become player-coach with Castleford. Mal was one of the new breed of coaches interested in developing their knowledge of fitness, diet, tactics, psychology and man-management. I had probably not spoken to him for longer than ten minutes in the whole of his career, but I knew that we would get on well together.

I called on Mal Reilly in his delightful old-world cottage in Ledsham, near Castleford. I explained that the post of Great Britain coach needed to be filled and that I intended to speak to two coaches to assess interest and suitability. Malcolm is a very reserved person, and on this occasion he was particularly cautious in our opening exchanges. When I invited him to express his views on our international standing he soon warmed to the task and shared his ideas on selection, preparation and commitment. I left impressed with his professionalism, his strong personality, firm opinions and clear leadership qualities.

Roger Millward had shown prodigious talent as a scrum-half, exhibiting extraordinary skills from an early age. He fulfilled his potential not with his home-town club Castleford, however, but with Hull KR. Roger was an international tourist who had played in Australia and eventually matured into a successful coach on Humberside. He had appeared at Wembley in 1986 as the rival coach to Mal Reilly, although on that occasion he came out second best. His pedigree was impeccable, ideally suited for the position of Great Britain coach.

Roger had a friendly, cheerful personality, and my contact with him at coaching conferences or during after-match chats reassured me that we would be able to strike up a partnership. He clearly wanted to be considered for the post of Great Britain coach, and I was soon engaged in a serious discussion about the problems we faced at international level and what

Malcolm Reilly was a 'hard man' loose forward for Castleford, Manly and Great Britain in the late 1960s and 1970s before returning to coach his home-town club, Castleford, to Wembley success in 1986. He was appointed Great Britain coach early in 1987.

needed to be done to remedy them. I came away from the meeting confident that he, too, was a suitable candidate and that both he and Malcolm would be acceptable to the Rugby Football League management board.

As I drove home I reflected on the respective merits of Mal Reilly and Roger Millward, trying to decide which one had the best credentials. They both fitted all the criteria, but my opinion began to swing in favour of Mal. It seemed to me that he was perfect for the job and that his time had come.

When I made my recommendation to the board I outlined the credentials of both candidates without stating my initial preference. Eventually opinion moved in favour of Mal Reilly and a unanimous decision was reached. Mal was contacted by telephone and he soon arrived at Chapeltown Road to be offered the position of Great Britain coach.

One of the first things we did was to drive over to Maurice Bamford's house where we were warmly received. Initially it had been thought appropriate that Maurice should continue as coach until after the next match against France, but Mal was keen to get down to business immediately and Maurice recognised the sense of that. A press conference was called for the following day and, after paying tribute to Maurice Bamford, I demonstrated my enthusiasm for Mal's appointment. Mal in turn expressed his delight at being asked to be Great Britain coach and immediately stated that Australia could be beaten and that he would apply himself to that end. He had played against them at Test level and alongside them in the Sydney League and he was not in awe of them.

A team now had to be selected for the forthcoming visit of France to Headingley on 24 January. Mal and I arranged to meet in Huddersfield for lunch and we soon arrived at a consensus on the best team. Injury ruled out Ward, Basnett and Myler and Andy Gregory was in dispute with his club, so we included Mark Forster of Warrington and Shaun Edwards in the backs, and David Hobbs, Kevin Beardmore, Mike Gregory and Roy Haggerty in the pack. Ellery Hanley was chosen as captain, a position he was to fill with distinction for years to come.

At the end of the meeting I raised the question of support staff, being careful to emphasise that Mal could bring in people that he preferred if necessary. Mal reassured me that he was not about to make changes for the sake of change, but he would meet with Phil Larder to see what they could work out. I wasn't present at the meeting but Mal rang me to say that they had got on very well and that he was happy for Phil to continue. There had been no pressure from me but I was quietly pleased that Mal had recognised Phil's qualities.

Mal's approach in camp was totally different to Maurice Bamford's, much more quiet and reserved, using words sparingly. His strong, fit appearance and his reputation as an outstanding player and 'hard man' gave him considerable presence. The players were very guarded, perhaps in awe of him, and they soon learnt to interpret a gesture or a look without him having to raise his voice. Right from day one Mal's authority was absolute.

Great Britain swept to a record-breaking 52–4 victory over France at Headingley, scoring nine tries and gaining two World Cup points. We played an expansive game and the French were unable to cope as Edwards revelled at scrum-half and Mike Gregory first gave notice that he was a future star, with two tries on his début. It was ironic that in both my first games with new coaches, Great Britain had scored 50 points at Headingley. I had a distinct feeling of *déjà vu* but had to remind myself that two years ago we were beaten in Perpignan in the return match. Could it happen again?

Great Britain: Lydon (Wigan); Forster (Warrington), Schofield (Hull), Stephenson (Wigan), Gill (Wigan); Hanley (Wigan), Edwards (Wigan); Hobbs (Oldham), Kevin Beardmore (Castleford), Crooks (Hull), Goodway (Wigan), Haggerty (St Helens), Mike Gregory (Warrington)
Substitutes: Creasser (Leeds) for Stephenson after 27 minutes, England (Castleford) for Hobbs after 62 minutes
Scorers: tries – Edwards (2), Mike Gregory (2), Hanley (2), Goodway, Lydon, Forster; goals – Lydon (8)

France: Perez; Couston, Palisses, Ratier, Pons; Espugna, Dumas; Storer, Mantese, Rabot, Verdes, Palanque, Bernabé

Substitutes: Rocci for Palisses after 16 minutes, Titeux for Dumas after 73 minutes

Scorer: goals – Perez (2)

Referee: M. Stone (Australia)

For the return match in Carcassonne on 8 February we kept changes to a minimum, recalling Andy Gregory at half-back and Chris Burton in the forwards, and giving Keith England a full match in the front row. There was some doubt that the match would ever take place up to four hours before kick-off. Internal politics had led to an emergency meeting of the French Federation which culminated in the sacking of their national coach, Tas Baitieri, and the suspension of their president, Jacques Soppelsa. There was a great deal of toing and froing by the Rugby Football League secretary-general, David Oxley, and chairman David Wigham with promises of financial support to offset a declared debt of £90,000. The French players

French prop Jean-Luc Rabot throws the punch that broke Mike Gregory's nose and cheek-bone in the ill-tempered encounter at Carcassonne in February 1987. Both players were sin-binned for their part in the brawl, although Gregory was unable to continue.

only agreed to play after an impassioned plea by Tas Baitieri and were clearly charged up when they took the field to defend the honour of France.

The match was a bad-tempered affair, refereed indifferently by leading Australian referee Mick Stone. The lowest point came when French prop forward Jean-Luc Rabot rushed in to punch Mike Gregory in the face, breaking his nose and cheek-bone. The referee decided to sin-bin them both, although Gregory never returned to the field of play. The French managed to disrupt Great Britain with tenacious tackling and in the end a disappointing 20–10 victory was achieved with tries from Beardmore, Hanley and Gill. Perhaps it was more important for the future of Rugby League in France that they had not conceded a large score because clearly the future of the game there was in jeopardy.

France: Perez; Berteloitte, Bienes, Moliner, Ratier; Espugna, Scicchitanno; Rabot, Trinque, Aillères, Verdes, Palanque, Bernabé
    Substitutes: Storer for Palanque after 71 minutes; Dumas not used
    Scorers: try – Espugna; goals – Perez (3)

Great Britain: Lydon (Wigan); Forster (Warrington), Schofield (Hull), Hanley (Wigan), Gill (Wigan); Edwards (Wigan), Andy Gregory (Wigan); Hobbs (Oldham), Kevin Beardmore (Castleford), England (Castleford), Burton (Hull KR), Haggerty (St Helens), Mike Gregory (Warrington)
    Substitutes: Dixon (Halifax) for Mike Gregory after 63 minutes; Stephenson (Wigan) not used
    Scorers: tries – Kevin Beardmore, Hanley, Gill; goals – Lydon (4)

Referee: M. Stone (Australia)

The whole trip was an excellent occasion for Mal, Phil and me to form strong bonds and to share our ideas on the way we should prepare for the 1988 tour to Australia. Mal was particularly keen to improve levels of fitness and strength, believing that we had skilful players but that their ability to compete at the highest physical and psychological level was in some doubt. The forthcoming close season was to be a critical period and a programme of conditioning needed to be mapped out. By now Rod Mckenzie had stepped down, and we decided to seek the advice of Wilf Paish, the former AAA national coach, who had a keen interest in Rugby League.

A squad of players was invited to attend for tests at Carnegie College, Leeds. Similar sessions had taken place in previous years, but the difference this time was that Mal, despite his damaged knee, was prepared to undertake the tests himself. All the results were recorded on individual player profile cards, but many players looked a little sheepish when Mal and Phil were among the leaders on the 12-minute run. In the gym, Mal was able to lift more weight than any other player. This, more than any other factor, acted as an incentive to those players who were under-achieving.

The track sessions were an essential part of Mal Reilly's new regime as players found they could not hide their levels of fitness from him even if they wanted to. There is no way that a player can cheat if asked to complete a series of sprints and runs with each one timed and recorded. The schedules varied and increased in intensity as the weeks progressed, and Shaun Edwards and Ellery Hanley invariably led the way and provided excellent role models. We knew that we had only a short period of time to make the necessary attitudinal change in the players so that they could be motivated to take responsibility for their own level of fitness.

During the autumn of 1987 Papua New Guinea visited Britain for a short tour. One of the matches was to be a full Test match against Great Britain for World Cup points. By now, Mal was the full-time Great Britain

Castleford's Kevin Ward enjoyed a magnificent series against the 1986 Kangaroos and went on to emerge as the world's leading prop forward with towering displays all over the world in the next two years. His sheer strength and ability to offload in the tightest of situations made him a genuinely feared opponent.

coach, having stepped down from his beloved Castleford position. I think he found it hard to adjust to his new responsibilities and he missed the regular contact with players that a club brings. Great Britain get-togethers are infrequent, and he now had to spend more time watching matches and videos to assess form. Phil Larder had devised a detailed match report sheet and various people were invited to complete these, focusing on one or two players. These provided an enormous bank of information for future reference.

The Kumuls were, to a certain extent, an unknown quantity, but their surprising 24–22 defeat of the Kiwis in Port Moresby in 1986 had put us right back into the running for the World Cup final. That victory also indicated that they could not be taken too lightly. When they defeated Featherstone 22–16 in the opening match of their tour and then went on to level the scores 22–22 against Lancashire we knew that we could not afford any complacency. They were skilful and elusive and were prepared to attack from anywhere.

Great Britain were without several players, unavailable for selection, and so we introduced Steve Hampson, Paul Groves and Paul Medley to the team, and moved Hanley to loose forward; there he joined the select band of players who have occupied four different berths in a Test team. The eight Wigan players in the team were the largest contingent from one club for thirty-seven years. Hanley and Phil Ford got Great Britain off to a flying start, and tries followed at regular intervals as the Kumuls failed to catch fire in the way that we had feared. Paul Medley gave hints of great promise for the future by scoring a début try and securing the man-of-the-match award in a comprehensive 42–0 victory.

Great Britain: Hampson (Wigan); Drummond (Warrington), Stephenson (Wigan), Lydon (Wigan), Phil Ford (Bradford Northern); Edwards (Wigan), Andy Gregory (Wigan); Ward (Castleford), Groves (St Helens), Case (Wigan), Goodway (Wigan), Medley (Leeds), Hanley (Wigan)
Substitutes: Woods (Warrington) for Lydon and Fairbank (Bradford Northern) for Medley after 65 minutes
Scorers: tries – Edwards (2), Phil Ford, Hanley, Medley, Lydon, Andy Gregory; goals – Stephenson (7)

Papua New Guinea: Kovae; Krewanty, Atoi, Numapo, Saea; Haili, Kila; Tep, Heni, Lomutopa, Kombra, Waketsi, Taumaku
Substitutes: Kitimun for Haili after 55 minutes, Gaius for Kombra after 70 minutes

Referee: F. Desplas (France)

In January 1988 we went to Avignon to play France with three new players in the squad: Hugh Waddell, a stocky prop from Oldham; Paul Loughlin, a powerful young centre from St Helens; and perhaps the most exciting newcomer, Martin Offiah. Doug Laughton had persuaded him to leave the Rosslyn Park Rugby Union club to join Widnes, and his impact on the game was dramatic and instantaneous as he scored tries with incredible regularity. Mal and Phil were a little sceptical about his defence but I convinced them to take the opportunity of looking at him. One omission, however, was Lee Crooks who had suffered a serious shoulder injury in the John Player Special Trophy semi-final when Leeds defeated Wigan. This injury was to prove far more costly to Great Britain than we realised at the time.

The French, under their new coach, Jacques Jorda, had been working desperately to put together a competitive team. There was an expectation that they would do better than in previous encounters. This indeed proved to be the case, in eighty minutes of fluent if flawed football. The French remained in sight of victory until the final minutes, when Hanley backed up substitute Dixon's burst and Schofield stole an interception to score the tries that took Great Britain clear by 28–14. Before then, however, Hanley had uncharacteristically spurned three try-scoring opportunities that would have put the seal on Drummond's dramatic eighty-metre effort and Edwards-inspired tries by Schofield and the débutant Offiah. A string of defensive errors kept the valiant and imaginative Frenchmen in the match at 18–14, until that late, crucial spurt by Great Britain.

France: Pougeau; Ratier, Delaunay, Fraisse, Pons; Espugna, Dumas; Tisseyre, Khedimi, Aillères, Montgaillard, Verdes, Moliner
Substitutes: Bienes for Fraisse after 50 minutes, Gestas for Moliner after 66 minutes
Scorers: tries – Verdes, Ratier; goals – Dumas (3)

Great Britain: Hampson (Wigan); Drummond (Warrington), Schofield (Leeds), Loughlin (St Helens), Offiah (Widnes); Hanley (Wigan), Edwards (Wigan); Ward (Castleford), Kevin Beardmore (Castleford), Waddell (Oldham), Roy Powell (Leeds), Medley (Leeds), Platt (St Helens)
Substitutes: Dixon (Halifax) for Medley after 65 minutes, Creasser (Leeds) for Loughlin after 71 minutes
Scorers: tries – Schofield (2), Drummond, Offiah, Hanley; goals – Loughlin (3), Creasser

Referee: N. Kesha (New Zealand)

During our time in Avignon the Great Britain management team met to discuss preparations for the Lions tour. To help the process, I had prepared a fairly detailed job specification for management members. I felt it was essential that we clarified exactly each person's responsibilities so that there would be no chance of overlap which could lead to tensions and conflict when we were a long way from home. Geoff Plummer, the physiotherapist, was given the task of ordering the equipment necessary to get us through a ten-week tour. Forbes Mackenzie, the first doctor ever to be chosen to accompany a Lions tour to Australasia, had already stocked up a supply of drugs and medicines. He was also charged with making arrangements for the various injections we would need for Papua New Guinea. Mal was particularly concerned about the problem of dehydration in PNG and was keen that the medical staff should provide plenty of vitamins and drinks containing essential minerals. Forbes was so professional in this area that he produced a paper on the whole topic which was a digest of existing research. Both the doctor and physio were assured that they would have the final word on fitness and that Mal and I would not overrule their recommendations. The amount of medical equipment we eventually took with us was enough to fill several large trunks.

Martin Offiah burst on to the Rugby League scene like a comet in 1987-88, having been snapped up by Widnes from Rosslyn Park Rugby Union club. The tries that he scored outweighed the early defensive frailties he betrayed, and he won his first cap in 1988 against France, scoring on his début.

David Howes, the recently appointed business manager, was in charge of financial matters and he was busy devising a system of accounting which would control the cash flow while we were away. He had also negotiated an extensive range of kit and equipment which we would receive before departure. I enjoyed our planning meeting and was instantly reassured with the enthusiasm and professionalism of everyone concerned. We had a good team, we got on well and there was mutual respect from everyone.

Although there were still a number of tour places up for grabs, Mal kept the changes for the return match with France on 6 February to a minimum. His most controversial move was the replacement of Offiah with David Plange, nominally as an experiment, while Paul Dixon replaced Paul Medley to stiffen the defensive resolve of the pack. Within five minutes Gregory and Hanley had crossed for tries, and the French were looking at a third consecutive 50-point drubbing in Leeds. However, hooker Khedimi made sure that France did not capitulate by holding Kevin Beardmore in the scrums and putting Cyrille Pons in for a try. Nonetheless, Great Britain added further tries through Hanley, Schofield and, after a fine move involving Gregory, Beardmore, Dixon and Schofield, the débutant Plange. It was fitting that Khedimi should have the last word for France, going over for a try that brought the score back to 30–12 and caused jubilation in the French dug-out.

The determination of Hugh Waddell to succeed in Rugby League was apparent from the day he walked into Blackpool Borough and asked for a trial. He was rewarded with his first cap in January 1988 and a place on the tour to Australia later that year.

Great Britain: Hampson (Wigan); Plange (Castleford), Schofield (Leeds), Hanley (Wigan), Phil Ford (Bradford Northern); Edwards (Wigan), Andy Gregory (Wigan); Ward (Castleford), Kevin Beardmore (Castleford), Waddell (Oldham), Roy Powell (Leeds), Dixon (Halifax), Platt (St Helens)
Substitutes: Medley (Leeds) for Roy Powell after 60 minutes, Stephenson (Leeds) for Edwards after 72 minutes
Scorers: tries – Andy Gregory, Hanley (2), Schofield, Plange; goals – Schofield (5)

France: Pougeau; Ratier, Fourquet, Delaunay, Pons; Espugna, Bourrel; Tisseyre, Khedimi, Aillères, Montgaillard, Verdes, Gestas
Substitutes: Moliner for Aillères after 52 minutes; Bienes not used
Scorers: tries – Pons, Khedimi; goals – Bourrel (2)

Referee: N. Kesha (New Zealand)

6

Launch of the Lions

After several meetings and many 'phone calls we met at the home of Forbes Mackenzie to select the 1988 Lions squad to tour Papua New Guinea, Australia and New Zealand. On 5 April we named twenty-four players:

Kevin Beardmore (Castleford)   Steve Hampson (Wigan)
Brian Case (Wigan)   Ellery Hanley (Wigan) capt
Paul Dixon (Halifax)   David Hulme (Widnes)
Shaun Edwards (Wigan)   Paul Loughlin (St Helens)
Karl Fairbank (Bradford Northern)   Joe Lydon (Wigan)
Michael Ford (Oldham)   Paul Medley (Leeds)
Phil Ford (Bradford Northern)   Martin Offiah (Widnes)
Henderson Gill (Wigan)   Andy Platt (St Helens)
Andy Goodway (Wigan)   Roy Powell (Leeds)
Andy Gregory (Wigan)   Garry Schofield (Leeds)
Mike Gregory (Warrington)   David Stephenson (Wigan)
Paul Groves (St Helens)   Kevin Ward (Castleford)

The three remaining places were to be filled from a training-on squad of nine. This included Lee Crooks, now back in the Leeds team following his serious shoulder injury, although there were serious doubts as to the extent of his recovery. His performances were indifferent and at training sessions he seemed to have some restriction in the full range of arm movement. Mal was confident, however, that the extra training Lee was putting in under his personal supervision would accelerate the rate of recovery, and that he would be match-fit for the first Test in June.

There was a similar doubt over Des Drummond who was on a course of intensive physiotherapy and fitness training to prove that his damaged knee would stand up to the stresses of the tour. It was decided to give him a little longer, and his specialist was confident that he would make the grade in time.

Overall we were happy with the squad, full of versatile and skilful players with an average age of 24. There was criticism that more Widnes players had not been selected and that there should have been room for giant props Brendan Hill and Kelvin Skerrett of Bradford Northern.

Widnes finished off the season by winning the Championship and the Premiership final, which brought our selection policy under the closest scrutiny. We considered that, although there were excellent players at Widnes, the key players were not superior to the ones we had selected.

Steve Hampson sustained a broken arm after the squad was announced which meant that our first choice full-back was out of contention. We hoped that he might recover sufficiently to fly out later in the tour; we did not announce an immediate replacement in the belief that in Loughlin and Lydon we had two potential full-backs.

The injury to Hampson was a major blow, but when we lost three more leading players soon afterwards I felt that someone was conspiring against us. When the squad met at Headingley for injections, measurement for blazers, passport details and the signing of contracts, Andy Goodway sought me out to explain that he was about to open a new restaurant in Chorley. This was a financial investment on his part to secure his future and he would need to be on hand to check progress. Andy was a vital part of our plans to beat Australia, and so I discussed the implications with Mal and David Howes and tried to come up with various strategies which would look after his business interests in his absence. In the end it was to no avail and Andy dropped out of the tour. The irony was that the project fell through and he never did open a restaurant, but his presence in Australia was sorely missed. As a replacement we selected Roy Haggerty from St Helens.

After more meetings and tests we decided to gamble on Lee Crooks recovering match fitness on tour. However, we also included Hugh Waddell, who had performed outstandingly well in the two France Tests, as cover. Ian Wilkinson of Halifax secured the final back position on account of his ability to play both full-back and centre.

Eight days before we were due to leave for Papua New Guinea I was returning from a match when I heard on the radio about a brawl at Naughton Park between Widnes and Warrington players. It was alleged that Des Drummond had been involved in an incident with a spectator. Within forty-eight hours Des Drummond and Joe Lydon, who had been awaiting sentence for a similar incident during a match against St Helens on Good Friday, were withdrawn from the tour by the Rugby Football League's management board.

Mal and I were rocked by this news as we felt it was a punishment out of proportion to the alleged offences. We did what we could over the telephone but were informed that the management board had taken legal advice and that they believed the course of action they had taken to be right and proper. Both Des and Joe were devastated and could not come to terms with the swiftness and savagery of the punishment. Des carries the hurt to this day, refusing to play for his country again.

Not only was it damaging to both players, it considerably reduced our firepower. I still reflect and wonder whether Australia would have withdrawn Wally Lewis and Gene Miles under similar circumstances.

In the Lions' Den

Perhaps I was too close to the situation to be totally objective, but within a period of three weeks one-third of our Test team – Hampson, Goodway, Drummond and Lydon – had been withdrawn. Because we had already planned to be without Lydon until after he had completed his exams we decided to call in only one replacement and settled on Carl Gibson of Leeds, a threequarter who was fourth in the season's try-scoring list.

Monday 16 May dawned bright and sunny, and the car park of the Bentley Arms, Rothwell, was a hive of activity as players arrived with their cases accompanied by mums, wives, sweethearts and children. A final meal, photos, speeches, kisses, waves of good-bye, shouts of good luck, tears, and we were on our way to Papua New Guinea, a remote, far-off place that most of us could not even find on the map.

We flew from Heathrow to Sydney via Bombay and Singapore. Forbes Mackenzie insisted that to combat jet-lag and to arrive in the best possible shape, no alcohol should be drunk and sleeping pills should be taken at prescribed times. The cabin crew thought we were a vicars' convention and remarked that we were the best behaved sports team they had ever known. From Sydney we flew to Brisbane and finally, two full days after leaving Rothwell, arrived in Port Moresby, Papua New Guinea.

As I left the plane I looked at the blue sky, estimated the temperature to be in the 90s and wondered how we would possibly play in such a humid temperature. Nonetheless, our hotel, the sumptuous Travel Lodge

Ellery Hanley, who first captained his country in 1985, was the first coloured sportsman ever to lead a Great Britain team on tour when he was given charge of the 1988 Lions party to Australia.

situated on a hill overlooking the harbour and bay, had air conditioning and a swimming pool, and I knew our stay was going to be very pleasant. The players were ordered to be changed and ready for training within twenty minutes, and the natives of Port Moresby must have been reminded of the old Noël Coward song *Mad Dogs and Englishmen* as Mal and Phil took them on an extended run. With a World Cup Test match scheduled for Sunday we only had three days to acclimatise and prepare.

We soon settled into the routine of touring and developed a healthy camaraderie among the squad. There was a social evening at the local brewery, a day at the races, a sportsman's lunch and a visit to the home of the High Commissioner for an evening barbecue. He and his wife had a splendid bungalow overlooking Port Moresby, and in the cool of the tropical evening we relaxed and met various members of the local community. Suddenly there was a splash and I turned to see Martin Offiah floating fully clothed in the pool. I hastened to reassure the High Commissioner that it was merely high spirits. His wife put me at my ease by saying that she was glad that the pool was being used, and Martin got his own back by launching several pairs of the players' shoes which they had discarded to cool off.

Each day we had a business meeting to co-ordinate arrangements for kit, food, training routine, social dates, dress, team meetings and so on, and a press conference. The press were with us all the time, sharing the hotel and joining in on various social jaunts, and were an integral part of the tour; they and their colleagues who joined us in Australia never abused this privilege. There was mutual trust, and I believe that this partnership is possibly unique in sport. They were there to report Rugby League and not seek out cheap sensationalism.

The day of the match turned out a little cooler with some breeze, and as we travelled to the ground there were plenty of smiles and waves from the open and friendly people of Port Moresby. Huge crowds had also travelled in from the country, and there were 12,000 packed into the tiny ground, many of them perched on the tin roof of the stand, up the scoreboard and on the branches of trees, Ellery Hanley instructed his team to run across the pitch and wave to the spectators. They loved this, cheered wildly and switched allegiance immediately. Ellery was adopted as their new chief.

In such an alien environment Mal had selected his most experienced team, the only gamble being the inclusion of young Paul Loughlin at full-back. It was only seven minutes, however, before Shaun Edwards limped out of the match and out of the tour with a torn medial ligament – another key player out of our plans. Great Britain rocketed into a 16-point lead, owing much to the prompting of Andy Gregory, and went in at half-time 28–6 ahead. However, the early exertions had taken their toll, and we had to wrap the players in wet towels stored in ice to offset the effects of heat exhaustion. The Kumuls came storming back after the interval with tries by their outstanding full-back Dairi Kovae, Krewanty and Rop, to narrow the score to 30–22, before David Stephenson, perhaps the worst affected by the heat, and Henderson Gill scored again to make the final margin 42–22 in Great Britain's favour. At the end of the day, it was colossal contributions from Hanley, Ward and Mike Gregory that held the side together.

Papua New Guinea: Kovae; Krewanty, Morea, Numapo, Saea; Haili, Kila; Bom, Malmillo, Rop, Kombra, Evei, Kovoru
Substitutes: Rombuk for Bom after 59 minutes, Lapan for Kombra after 77 minutes
Scorers: tries – Kovae (2), Krewanty, Rop; goals – Numapo (3)

Great Britain: Loughlin (St Helens); Phil Ford (Bradford Northern), Schofield (Leeds), Stephenson (Leeds), Gill (Wigan); Edwards (Wigan), Andy Gregory (Wigan); Ward (Castleford), Kevin Beardmore (Castleford), Case (Wigan), Medley (Leeds), Mike Gregory (Warrington), Hanley (Wigan)
Substitutes: David Hulme (Widnes) for Edwards after 7 minutes, Dixon (Halifax) for Case after 34 minutes
Scorers: tries – Schofield (2), Gill (2), Medley, Mike Gregory, Stephenson; goals – Loughlin (7)

Referee: G. McCallum (Australia)

We had one more game in Papua New Guinea, against a Highland Districts XIII, which would enable the second string to show their paces. At the rate we were losing players, however, it was becoming difficult to say who our second string were. Many of the players picked up serious grass burns which turned septic and meant that training was painful as the inflamed scabs split open when they ran. We flew across the island to Lae which is situated close to a tropical palm beach. On landing we were whisked to a four-star luxury hotel with air conditioning to relax until kick-off. The players changed in rooms set aside and travelled to the ground ready to play. Once again, the ground was packed, and at one stage during the match there was a loud crack as a huge branch gave way under the weight of spectators. Fortunately no one was hurt and we went on to win 36–18. Martin Offiah scored a hat-trick of tries, and we were relieved to see Lee Crooks emerge from the match unscathed.

The next stop was Cairns in Northern Queensland, where we stayed at the Tradewinds Esplanade Hotel; for the players it was a glimpse of paradise. It was superbly appointed, situated on the sea front with excellent services. The players seemed happier in an Australian setting and morale was high. Twice daily training sessions at 8.00 a.m. and 3.30 p.m. were instituted, as Mal still wanted to raise fitness levels. However, he did express some concern at the error rate in the skills drills that were part of his training routine. Nonetheless, we defeated Northern Queensland by

66–16, the highest score by a touring side in twenty-six years, with Martin Offiah notching a further four tries.

The following day the whole party went on a compulsory trip to the Great Barrier Reef. Back in England we had decided to avoid some of the pitfalls of previous tours, such as leaving players to their own devices; all too often this can lead to boredom and the formation of cliques. We sailed out to the Barrier Reef and moored against a huge pontoon. Everyone was free to don flippers and masks to explore the sea-bed, and there was a glass-bottomed boat for the older people to get a clear view of the mysteries of the deep. One of the crew asked me to stop the players diving off the top of the boat because of the potential danger. When I got to the top deck no one was to be seen except Mal, who looked very sheepish when I told him what some of the players had been doing. 'I know,' he said, 'I was the first one to dive off.'

If the players let their hair down on their free day Mal certainly made them pay for it at the 8:00 a.m. training session the following day, where one or two struggled to keep up. Mal used the session to reinforce the message that anyone who was not up to his demanding fitness schedules would be shown no mercy. We were here to win matches and a player's social life would not, under any circumstances, be allowed to jeopardise the success of the tour. A few players came of age that morning.

In a sense, the time spent in Papua New Guinea and Cairns was our honeymoon period. Although being part of a British Lions tour is for many the realisation of a sporting dream, its rarefied atmosphere makes considerable demands on one's social skills. Living constantly in an all-male environment, having to keep to routines of training, meals, matches, meetings and functions can be a recipe for disaster if people don't get on. As management, we were constantly vigilant for signs of homesickness, isolation, tension, emotional outbursts, indiscipline or low morale. Problems can arise when individual players suffer loss of form, receive injury or are not selected, and a certain amount of 'tea and sympathy' needs to be administered by the coaching or medical staff.

By contrast our arrival in Sydney went off like a damp squib. Bob Abbott, the secretary of the Australian Rugby League, was the only official to meet us at the airport, and the press had already left for Brisbane for the next State of Origin match between Queensland and New South Wales. The official press call and welcome was scheduled for the following day but once again there were apologies from the Australian officials for the marked absence of the media. David Howes, our business manager, was already expressing concern at the low level of promotion of the Centenary Test between Great Britain and Australia in this bicentennial year.

At the official lunch there were the usual welcoming speeches, and I responded on behalf of the Lions. The guests seemed to think we lacked size and bulk but I responded by saying that we were lean and hungry like dogs of war ready to be unleashed. I pointed out that there was a marked

Andy Gregory was perhaps the most important player on the 1988 Lions tour of Australia, and the Wigan scrum-half enjoyed an outstanding Test series.

absence of flab and there were no beer bellies, since I was determined to challenge the deprecatory view of British Rugby League players that seemed to prevail in Australia.

We had three days before we were due to play Newcastle Knights, an emerging team in the Sydney League. Facilities in our Manly base were excellent, and training in sunshine gave an enormous psychological boost to all of us. As part of the preparation we tuned in to the State of Origin match on TV so that the intensity of Australian rugby could be brought home to the players. The match was tough and competitive and at times the pressure unrelenting, and Mal and Phil were able to put this to good effect in their build-up to the match against Newcastle.

Newcastle is an industrial community and a large crowd was expected. In the event the day of the match was wet and only 8,000 spectators turned out. We won 28–12, which was reasonably convincing, although there was a worrying spell mid-game when defensive lapses pulled the score back to 12–12. There were good signs, however, as Andy Gregory, Kevin Ward, Ellery Hanley, Paul Dixon and Mike Gregory staked their claims for Test places. We were also pleased to see that Paul Loughlin playing at full-back was maturing into a fine player, while Martin Offiah scored twice to take his tally to nine in three matches on tour.

After the Newcastle match we discussed the idea of not playing certain key players until the first Test match. The rationale behind this was that we simply could not risk them picking up injuries; we had to field our best side against Australia, and already several players we had banked on were back in England and unavailable. Phil Larder recommended putting the key players on a special fitness schedule that he would personally supervise twice a day, which would include weights, sprints and interval runs up to 200 metres. Players who came into this category were Hanley, Andy Gregory, Ward, Beardmore, Mike Gregory, Dixon, Platt and Schofield.

We flew to Tamworth, a small country town, for our match against Northern Division feeling confident. The press were taking bets on the number of points we would score over 30, and although there had been torrential rain we were fairly relaxed. We were humiliated 12–36; the Lions biggest defeat in Australia outside the Tests for sixty-eight years. Mal, Phil and myself had expressions on our face that said it all. The players were silent and Mal kept them in the dressing-room for half an hour after the match. Our policy of sheltering the better players looked fairly shallow, while David Hulme's low-key performance in Shaun Edwards's stead at stand-off and Lee Crooks's sluggish showing in the pack were doubly disappointing.

Our next match was against Manly, currently at the top of the Sydney League, on the Tuesday evening before the first Test. Our key players were still under wraps, but we still expected to be competitive and used the heavy defeat at Tamworth as a warning. Playing at Manly was special for Mal because of his glory days as a player with the club in the 1970s.

Everywhere he went in the town he was recognised, and Manly supporters would seek him out to remind him of the old days.

Unhappily for Mal, the match was another disappointment as we stumbled from one mistake to another. There was a large crowd, many of them British, and a good atmosphere, but our players seemed unable to compete and we went down 0–30. Manly, with Noel Cleal, Cliff Lyons and an outstanding young half-back, Geoff Toovey, were a fine side, but we finally realised that our midweek team could not survive without the assistance of half a dozen of the Test squad.

A press conference was called for 5:30 p.m. the next day, when the Test team was to be announced. We went into the meeting feeling positive and emphasised that we had come to win the Ashes and, up to date in Australia, our best team had not been on show. The team we selected was a fit and mobile team and experienced enough to bring off a shock. The only surprise was Paul Dixon out of position at prop; here we were going for Paul's mobility and tackle rate. David Hulme was selected at stand-off to play opposite the great Wally Lewis. David was not a player with the overall skill of the injured Shaun Edwards but he was competitive, aggressive and a winner.

We had our final training session on the Friday at the superbly appointed ground of North Sydney, also a cricket club with splendid Edwardian stands. No advertising is allowed in the ground and, all in all, it is one of the most delightful sporting arenas I have ever visited. For the rest of the day I played nine holes of golf with Forbes Mackenzie and former Great Britain full-back Paul Charlton. Paul had been Salford's full-back when I was coach, and was a fellow Cumbrian. He had recently emigrated to Australia and, like many of the other exiled Brits in Sydney, popped over to wish us well.

Saturday 11 June dawned brightly. I was soon fielding 'phone calls from the Australian press, and one which I was pleased to receive from John Burgess, manager of the England Rugby Union team who were also touring Australia, to wish us well. All the same, the morning of the match dragged slowly with everyone trying to conceal their nervousness. Kevin Ward plunged into the sea believing it would bring him luck, as twelve months earlier he had been a member of Manly's successful Grand Final team and had swum on the morning of the match; was it an omen?

We journeyed to the stadium, each of us deep in his own thoughts. Mal looked particularly tense, as for him it was to be the first critical examination of his coaching ability at international level. So much was expected of him, and yet he had only been in charge for seventeen months. If he was apprehensive about the outcome then he certainly did not express any misgivings. His team were fit and, although it was not the team he had expected back in England to select, the hard work each player had put in to justify selection was a strong bonus.

The atmosphere in the dressing-room was reassuring as the players moved about in a confident and resolute manner. Captain Hanley rapped out frequent reminders to the team: 'Keep your discipline'; 'Control the ball'; 'Play in their half'; 'No high tackles'; 'Support the break'; 'Do not hang off Lewis or Sterling'. Eventually Mal and Phil had had their final say and it was time to move out.

There were 22,000 spectators in the new Sydney Football Stadium which Maurice Bamford and I had seen being constructed in 1986. This was the first Test match to be played there rather than in the Sydney Cricket Ground, but still the stadium was only half-full. Australian promotion of the match had been poor, but we had not done ourselves any favours with our recent performances.

The opening exchanges surpassed our wildest dreams. Diligently served by Beardmore and Andy Gregory, Kevin Ward time and again battered his way through tackles, while his pack colleagues Dixon, Platt, Mike Gregory and Hanley rocked the Australians back on their heels with a succession of resounding tackles. Loughlin's immaculate punting made sure that play remained deep in the Australian half but, with four minutes to go before half-time, all that Great Britain had to show for their overwhelming superiority was a 2–0 lead. Then, from an attack built up on the left-hand touchline, the ball was transferred quickly across the field to Hulme, whose sweet short ball put Hanley on an unstoppable run to the corner. The relief at turning pressure into points was matched only by the sight of Peter Sterling, Australia's dynamo, in considerable distress as a result of coming between Hanley and the line.

The scene in the dressing-room at half-time was pandemonium as the coaching staff tried to calm everyone down. Emotion and passion were running high and everyone was talking at once. The trouble was that the excitement was draining away adrenalin and energy faster than the game. Mal finally got the team quiet but the players' eyes were blazing and it was impossible for them to be totally rational – they believed they could win.

The second half, however, was not quite like the first and slowly but surely Lewis and the patched-up Sterling began to prod Australia back to life. In the forty-ninth minute Sterling, on the sixth tackle, attempted a short, stabbing grubber-kick for the line. In fact he miskicked and the ball only went three feet to his left, but it totally wrong-footed our defence. As he swooped to regather it Sam Backo arrived on his shoulder to take a short pass and crash through Hanley's tackle over the line. The score remained at 6–6 until sixteen minutes from the end when, after concerted Australian pressure, Sterling held up the final pass to put Peter Jackson over for a try.

Great Britain were not finished yet, and Andy Gregory crossed the line from a short run-around pass from Kevin Ward, a favourite set move christened 'Wardy'. But the pass was ruled forward and the try disallowed;

but if the execution of the move had been technically a little more accurate we would have been back on level terms.

Hanley (right) and Offiah celebrate in typical fashion after the former has given Great Britain the lead in the first Australian Test of 1988. The backdrop of the empty stand is a sad comment on the Australian marketing of the match.

After a drop-goal by Lewis, Australia finally pulled away with an excellent try from Jackson, worked by Lewis and Lindner. The move highlighted one of the few occasions when our defence had been found wanting, not least that of Martin Offiah, whose inexperience exposed him several times. This time he missed his opposing wingman, Andrew Ettingshausen, twice which launched the try-scoring move. Australia were flattered by their final victory margin of 17–6.

Australia: Jack; Ettingshausen, O'Connor, Jackson, Currie; Lewis, Sterling; Backo, Conescu, Phil Daley, Fullerton-Smith, Vautin, Lindner
Substitutes: Folkes for Vautin after 70 minutes, Belcher for Sterling after 75 minutes
Scorers: tries – Backo, Jackson (2); goals – O'Connor (2); drop-goal – Lewis

Great Britain: Loughlin (St Helens); Phil Ford (Bradford Northern), Schofield (Leeds), Stephenson (Leeds), Offiah (Widnes); David Hulme (Widnes), Andy Gregory (Wigan); Ward (Castleford), Kevin Beardmore (Castleford), Dixon (Halifax), Platt (St Helens), Mike Gregory (Warrington), Hanley (Wigan)
Substitutes: Roy Powell (Leeds) for Mike Gregory after 70 minutes, Gill (Wigan) for Loughlin after 78 minutes
Scorers: try – Hanley; goal – Loughlin

Referee: F. Desplas (France)

The despair in our dressing-room was etched on every player's face as they sat slumped and inconsolable. Kevin Ward, who had had an epic game to win the man-of-the-match award, was drained of all energy – he had just played the game of his life and it was still not enough. The players knew – we all knew – that the game could have been won.

Mal was bitterly disappointed, but knew that the manner of our defeat put the tour back on the road and there would be renewed interest in the second Test in Brisbane. The Lions were roaring again. Our bad luck returned to haunt us, however, when Dr Mackenzie confirmed that Andy Platt, one of the successes of the tour, had broken a bone in his wrist.

We left for Brisbane the following day. The players were given a night off to relax and enjoy themselves but we sensed that there was some slackness appearing in their general conduct which, if allowed to go unchecked, could give grounds for concern. Next day Mal gave them one of his punishing 8:00

Watched by captain Hanley, Kevin Ward ignores the attentions of Wally Lewis (No. 6) and Greg Conescu (No. 9) to unload the ball to Andy Gregory during the first Australian Test of 1988. Ward played the match of his life on this occasion, yet he could not bring victory to the Lions.

a.m. training sessions from which there was no hiding, and then we called a special team meeting after breakfast. We thanked the players for their performance in the Test match, and reminded them of the job still to be done and cautioned them against their social life jeopardising their playing performance. The players got the message, and to reinforce it several key players were invited to a private meeting with Mal and myself so that we could seek their opinions and enlist their aid in providing leadership and discipline.

We were due to play a Combined Brisbane XIII at Lang Park two days after our arrival there. In the old days this would have been a plum fixture, but the creation of the Brisbane Broncos and their entry into the Sydney League has knocked the bottom out of the Brisbane competition in terms of quality and spectator appeal. The Brisbane League has virtually become a nursery for professional clubs in Sydney and its future is in serious question. When we discovered that our match was also to be televised we feared the worst.

Only 1,800 paying customers turned out for our first match in Brisbane following our stirring performance in the Test. This was a pathetic turn-out and brought into sharp focus the fixture programme of future tours. Traditionally tours have always started in Northern Queensland with a selection of up-country matches against district or regional sides. The purpose of these matches was originally to promote Rugby League, but with modern travel and television the validity of such missionary work has to be questioned. On top of that modern touring is expensive. In effect we were losing money to play these matches, in order to subsidise the promotion of Rugby League in Australia.

We won the match against Combined Brisbane 24–14 but Garry Schofield sustained a fractured cheek-bone. That night at a sombre management meeting we reviewed the situation. Schofield would have to return home after an operation scheduled for the following day, and we decided that Paul Medley should accompany him. So much had been expected of Paul with his superb physique and running ability, but a loss of confidence followed by a serious neck injury convinced us that he was unlikely to recover in time. In addition Mike Ford had sustained a broken hand, David Stephenson a dead leg, and Brian Case needed eight stitches to a head wound. We were now down to fifteen fit players, so David Howes was asked to arrange for Andy Currier and Paul Hulme of Widnes to be flown out as replacements. Their club-mate Darren Wright had already joined the tour as an early replacement for Shaun Edwards.

With one win already under our belt in Brisbane we were anxious to win our next three matches, against Central Queensland, Toowoomba and Wide Bay. We achieved our objective but once again picked up a few more serious injuries. Lee Crooks lasted for only seven minutes of the 64–8 romp against Central Queensland, and David Stephenson, falling heavily on his shoulder, and Ian Wilkinson failed to survive the 28–12 win over

Toowoomba. Consequently the biggest satisfaction of the 14–0 win over Wide Bay was not the completion of a quartet of wins, but that everyone remained intact.

As for Andy Gregory – well that's another story. Andy had sustained a wound to his index finger which required eight stitches. Andy's explanation, that he had caught it in the lift door, was less than convincing. This meant that he couldn't play in the first two matches in Brisbane. He eventually declared himself fit for the third match but rather than risk possible damage to the finger in the final training session Mal ordered him to go on a run while the rest of the team played touch football. Imagine our despair when we returned to the hotel to find Andy had pulled a hamstring on the run. There was probably a funny side to it but no one was laughing – least of all Andy.

Forbes McKenzie and Geoff Plummer, the physiotherapist, worked round the clock on the injured players but time seemed to be running out before the second Test. In fact a rumour got back to England that so serious was the injury problem that I had arranged trials for the press. This lighthearted rumour came about because I organised an impromptu challenge match of touch football in which such stars as Ray French (BBC), Brian Batty (*Daily Mail*), Alan Thomas (*Daily Express*), Paul Wilson (*Independent*), Keith Macklin (*The Times*), Martin Richards (*Daily Mirror*), Stuart Pyke (Radio Piccadilly), Paul Harrison (*Sun*), and John Robinson (*People*) did their best to impress me – needless to say they did not.

Although an X-ray had revealed a flaked bone in Andy Platt's wrist the hope was that he would recover in time and that with the aid of a pain-killing injection he would be able to play in the Test. There was no doubt that his wrist was very painful but the bone was non-weight-bearing, and a second opinion from an Australian specialist confirmed that, with padding and strapping, no further damage was likely to occur. In the end the decision was Andy's and we believed it was a legitimate risk to take.

Mental attitude features more in the preparation of some players than others. Ellery Hanley possesses the natural gift of being able to direct his mental energy to achieve his goal, able to switch on and switch off his concentration. He actually professes never to worry about a game – his self-belief is total. I mention this because he objected strongly to attending a special function arranged by the Australian High Commissioner several days before the second Test. The function was also attended by the Australian squad and Ellery and some of the players felt that socialising with the enemy was the wrong thing to do. Ellery stayed for the minimum amount of time and then left with a small group of players who shared similar views. They would not be persuaded that a social event five days before a Test match was hardly likely to affect the result.

During our time in Brisbane we had been given permission to use the extensive playing facilities of a nearby public school. When we arrived for the final session before the Test match, however, we were involved in an incident that made exactly the wrong kind of headlines in the local press. Every year the school hosted a Rugby Union coaching camp which was scheduled to begin that morning. The school thought that we knew, but we assumed it wasn't due to begin until the afternoon. Despite our efforts to persuade the chief coach to release a pitch we had to depart in disarray. It was a minor inconvenience and we soon organised taxis to take us to a local rugby club – but it wasn't the ideal way to prepare.

In selecting our Test line-up we decided to make a number of positional changes from the first Test. Schofield and Stephenson were both injured, so we moved Hanley and Phil Ford into the centre. We felt that Hanley's defensive qualities were needed to contain Australia's attack out wide, but moving Ford was a calculated gamble. He had never played centre before but he was enjoying a splendid tour and his elusive ability could prove to be a secret weapon. We moved big Roy Powell into the front row and selected a back three of Platt, Dixon and Mike Gregory. All in all the pack looked strong although we still had grave reservations about Andy Platt's wrist.

Lang Park is one of the great Rugby League arenas, and at 7:30 p.m. on Tuesday 28 June it was packed with 30,000 spectators including a sizeable crowd of British supporters who had saved up their money to make the trip of a lifetime.

Our dressing-room was more aggressive than any dressing-room I had known in my time as manager. Players were wound up like coiled springs, as if they were going into war, which was not something the coaches had planned. Being psyched up is one thing, but if it's all left behind in the dressing-room or expended in the opening exchanges then it's a recipe for disaster. Energy needs to be conserved and used for eighty minutes, and a good team plays with its head as much as its heart. Aggression has an important part to play in a collision sport like Rugby League, but calm, steely determination is preferable to wild-eyed aggression; at Lang Park we seemed to have the latter.

The Australians were to complain afterwards that our aggression manifested itself in a savage, head-hunting assault on the field, but it would be fair to say that, in a tempestuous, ill-humoured match, they gave as good as they got. But Great Britain's indiscipline spread from their temper to their tackling, passing and kicking, with the result that they failed to put Australia under pressure for any length of time. Nowhere were their failings better illustrated than in Phil Ford's wild, arm-swinging tackle on Michael O'Connor in the sixth minute, which the centre ducked before racing clear to the line. Wally Lewis then took a hand in affairs, putting through an immaculate chip kick for Peter Jackson to score and then producing two superb dummies in a move that put Andrew Ettingshausen in at the corner.

The match was over at half-time, the Australian forwards overwhelming the British six in which Paul Dixon battled on gamely with a broken thumb, but Andy Platt failed to justify our gamble. The truth of this was underscored by close-range forward's tries from Sam Backo and Wayne Pearce and, although Hanley broke through to put Phil Ford away and Martin Offiah showed a gorgeous glimpse of his try-scoring speed, a final flourish by Lewis gave Australia a 34–14 victory which they fully deserved. Without cohesion, composure or control, Great Britain were a grave disappointment.

Lions captain Ellery Hanley, switched to the centre for the second Test in Brisbane in 1988, is tackled by Australia's Wayne Pearce as Henderson Gill arrives in support.

Australia: Jack; Ettingshausen, O'Connor, Jackson, Currie; Lewis, Sterling; Backo, Conescu, Phil Daley, Fullerton-Smith, Vautin, Pearce
Substitutes: Lindner for Conescu after 68 minutes, Belcher for Ettingshausen after 74 minutes
Scorers: tries – O'Connor, Jackson, Ettingshausen, Backo, Pearce, Lewis; goals – O'Connor (5)

Great Britain: Loughlin (St Helens); Gill (Wigan), Phil Ford (Bradford Northern), Hanley (Wigan), Offiah (Widnes); David Hulme (Widnes), Andy Gregory (Wigan); Ward (Castleford), Kevin Beardmore (Castleford), Roy Powell (Leeds), Dixon (Halifax), Platt (St Helens), Mike Gregory (Warrington)
Substitutes: Paul Hulme (Widnes) for Platt after 51 minutes, Wright (Widnes) for Phil Ford after 69 minutes
Scorers: tries – Phil Ford, Offiah; goals – Loughlin (3)

Referee: F. Desplas (France)

The players trooped back to the dressing-room drained and ashamed. Mal summed it up when he said to the press, 'I was expecting more – it just wasn't there.' He offered no explanation and he refused any words of comfort or consolation. Mal is a proud man and his pride was hurt, but it was his team and he had no intention of kicking them now that they were down.

Next day the papers crucified us and were particularly incensed at what they considered to be our dirty play. The *Sydney Daily Mirror* shrieked, 'Bloody Revenge – We'll Smash the Poms to Pieces Next Time.' Peter Frilingos, a particularly vitriolic writer, wrote, 'Vengeful Australian players are threatening to turn the third Test into a bloodbath.'

While we were prepared to accept responsibility for some indisciplined play from one or two players, this sensational reporting by the Australian media was ludicrous – but then they had a lot of column inches to fill. The campaign was so hysterical that when we arrived in Sydney Ken Arthurson, the Australian Rugby League chairman, felt it necessary to call a meeting of the Great Britain and Australian management. The Australian coach, Don Furner, was compelled to fly in from Canberra for a summit meeting designed to calm us down; in fact it achieved the opposite effect. We knew what our responsibilities were and we didn't need to be reminded about clamping down on dirty play. As far as we were concerned head shots from Conescu and Lewis had gone unpunished, and in the first Test a vicious tackle by Daley on Beardmore had seemed a sending-off offence. Mal was not pleased and was very concerned that pressure would be brought to bear on the French referee, Francis Desplas. We were worried that Desplas, who had been heavily criticised by the media for his performance in both Tests, might overreact and penalise us for any tackle above the knee.

At the next management meeting we reviewed the situation and decided that because of their injuries Paul Dixon and Andy Platt would have to return home but we would not seek replacements. Twenty-four hours later we changed our minds. This volte-face was caused by Lee Crooks. Mal had shown great loyalty to Lee, but the medical staff had always expressed strong doubts because they knew that Lee had nerve damage to the shoulder joint which meant that no amount of training would speed up the healing process.

Lee had worked hard on his fitness but when he received another knock to his shoulder causing pins and needles even Mal had to admit defeat. It was clear that Lee would not be able to contribute further and should join Andy Platt and Paul Dixon on the flight home.

We decided to send for Richard Eyres of Widnes and John Joyner of Castleford. John was a seasoned campaigner who had served Mal well in the past and had been on two previous tours. Mal felt that his experience would be invaluable.

Public interest in the third Test was very poor, and the number of advance tickets sold indicated the likelihood of an all-time low Test crowd. Bob Abbott, the secretary of the Australian Rugby League, was quoted as saying, 'Promoting Great Britain is like flogging a dead horse.' This screamed out from newspaper headlines, and when the TV cameras were pointed in my direction with a microphone under my nose I retorted that, 'It is our job to play Rugby League and Bob Abbott's job to help promote the game. If this is the best he can come up with, then in my view it is a pretty pathetic effort.' Ken Arthurson, the Australian chairman, rang me up to apologise and suggested that Bob had been quoted out of context. Bob Abbott is an experienced official and a pleasant guy, but I suspect the unfortunate 'flogging a dead horse' remark slipped out in a unwary moment.

Although the squad was working hard, a 28–26 win over a weak Western Division did little to lift our confidence, and on the Tuesday before the third Test we had the daunting prospect of playing a President's XIII in Canberra. This was in effect Australia's second team and bristled with such names as Mal Meninga, Greg Alexander, Glenn Lazarus, David Gillespie, Mark Geyer and Gavin Miller who had an opportunity to catch the selectors' eye. We came away from the match with some credit and came within a shout of winning it, with two spectacular long-range tries from Phil Ford in the unaccustomed position of full-back. A last-minute score by the President's XIII made the score 16–24 but Richard Eyres, Ward, Mike Gregory and Waddell had outstanding games. Unfortunately we picked up more injuries.

It was in Canberra that David Stephenson expressed the view that the management had not given the players enough free time. I explained to David that our policy of restricted free time was deliberate but I accepted the view he expressed. It is probably a better policy to identify free days well in advance so that players have something to look forward to. I raised the matter with the coaches and although we couldn't do anything about what had already happened there was probably some sense in giving the squad the next day off, even though the Test match was only three days away.

Training was scheduled for 10:00 a.m. the day before the Test, and the press turned out in force in anticipation of the announcement of the Great Britain team. An impromptu meeting of the Great Britain management delayed training for fifteen minutes as we decided on the best course of action. Six players in contention for the match were unable to train and required treatment. Kevin Ward was complaining of pain in his ankle and was convinced that he had a stress fracture. Richard Eyres had a swollen knee. Kevin Beardmore had sustained heavy bruising to his hip in the Canberra match, and his deputy, Paul Groves, had a badly bruised big toe. Andy Gregory, with a hamstring strain, and Mike Gregory, with a groin strain, were not capable of undertaking two training sessions that day. It was decided to delay a final decision to the afternoon.

None of the press bothered to turn up for the afternoon training session, concluding that we were a lost cause. The final medical report was both good and bad. An X-ray on Ward's ankle had revealed nothing so at least he was psychologically reassured. Both Gregorys had had intensive

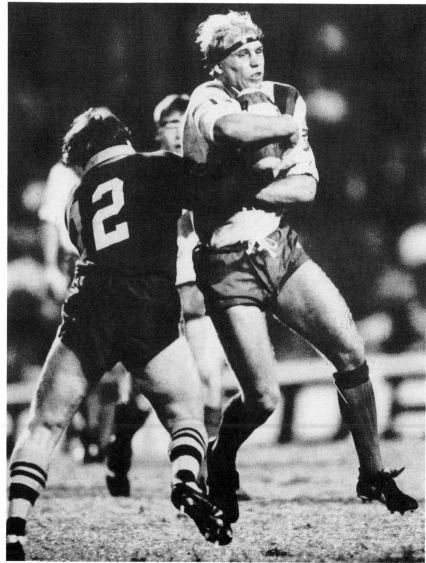

Warrington's Mike Gregory, driving through the tackle of Paul Vautin, came of age on the 1988 Lions tour to establish himself as one of the world's premier back-rowers. His try in the third Test victory at Sydney lives long in the memory of those who saw it.

treatment but it was doubtful whether either of them would finish the game. Beardmore, Groves and Eyres were ruled out, so we decided to play Paul Hulme at hooker, a position he had never played in his life. He was a mobile loose forward who had regularly filled the role of scrum-half at Widnes. The number of scrums would be negligible, and we needed someone capable of controlling the game from acting half-back. The front row was completed by Hugh Waddell, due reward for all the work and effort he had put in throughout the tour.

Before that final training session Mal made strong, positive statements about what was expected of the players. He told them that he had unreserved faith in them and that victory was still possible. He particularly emphasised how fit they were and how much work they had put in. The players in turn reaffirmed their commitment, and the practice was sharp and error-free, everyone going through the drills with total concentration. I knew then that we were not in as bad a shape as everyone else believed: John Hogan of the *Australian* had announced that it was a 'Sham Test' and predicted a record score, while the rest of the Sydney press played variations on the same theme: we were no-hopers.

The journey to the Sydney Football Ground on Saturday 9 July was in the quietest team coach I have ever experienced in all my years as player, coach and manager. Even the press who travelled with us were silent, and although I sat next to Mal we did not speak. The silence continued in the dressing-room. It was quite unnerving, and Phil Larder expressed his unease to me, interpreting the mood as that of the condemned man in his cell.

Andy Gregory was the first one to spark into life and exhorted the players to start talking and to get some spirit. I remember him going over to Roy Powell – a gentle, quiet man who was an ideal tourist – cuffing him across the head and saying, 'Now then, big fella, let's get mean and rip some heads off today.' Slowly but surely commitment and passion were built up in different ways, and the atmosphere became electric.

Mal did not say much before the match as all of us had had our say in previous team meetings. He got the players to sit down and concentrate for a few minutes, and reminded them why we were all there; about the insults we had had to endure from the Australian press; about the fact that people back in England would be switching on their TVs, that there were thousands of Brits in the stadium, and that they carried the hopes and aspirations of the whole of British Rugby League. 'Believe in yourself,' he said. 'Believe in your team-mates, stick to the game plan, and you will win.'

Just before the players left the dressing-room, the captain, Ellery Hanley, paused at the door, looked back and said, 'Remember: no sorrys. I don't want to hear anybody say, "I'm sorry, I made a mistake; I'm sorry, I'm tired; I'm sorry, I'm injured; I'm sorry, I missed a tackle" – NO sorrys. If I hear any sorrys, don't bother coming back at half-time. Let's go out and win.'

The opening exchanges were tough and uncompromising, with Waddell a revelation on his Ashes début and Ward and Powell driving strongly, backed up by the industrious Paul Hulme. But an early chance went begging when referee Desplas mysteriously disallowed a try after Phil Ford had followed through to claim a lofted kick by Andy Gregory which was horribly misjudged by Australian full-back Garry Jack. We could not believe our ill fortune, particularly when Australia stormed back and hooker Conescu was twice held up over the line on his back.

Great Britain's defence held, however, and slowly Andy Gregory and David Hulme began to turn the match. After sixteen minutes Gregory and Kevin Ward put on their party piece, 'Wardy', and this time the return pass was timed to perfection. Gregory shot through a gap and, fractionally before being tackled, lobbed a pass out to wingman Offiah, who sprinted into the corner. If our spirits were raised by this, they were sent soaring four minutes later when Andy Gregory, having the match of his life, followed strong work by Mike Gregory and Paul Hulme to put Phil Ford through a gap in midfield. Ford still had plenty to do, but his mazy run took him under the posts, and Great Britain in at half-time 10–0 to the good.

This time the mood in the dressing-room was more controlled, but that didn't stop Wally Lewis, now shorn of his sparring partner Sterling, getting a hold of events early in the second half, just as he had done in the first Test. Storming through the tackles of Paul Hulme and Waddell, he evaded Phil Ford's outstretched arms and crashed between the posts for a brilliant solo try. With Australia back to 10–6, it could all have been *déjà vu*. But this time Great Britain stepped up their efforts, and six minutes later it was Andy Gregory again, chipping through with precision for Henderson Gill to race behind the hesitant Jack and Jackson for the score.

It was Australia's turn to rally again, and big Sam Backo powered over for his third try of the series to pull the score back to 16–12. But Great Britain were not to be denied, and Paul Loughlin, back in his favoured centre position, broke from his own 22-metre area in a surging run. Although his pass out to Gill was a little early, the winger slipped comfortably round Garry Jack and went in at the corner. His celebration jig was to become one of the great moments in British sport.

Nine minutes from the end Great Britain wrapped it up, and it was that man Andy Gregory who sold an outrageous dummy only fifteen metres from his own posts, sped through a gap and put his namesake Mike on a 75-metre charge to the line. In 1982 and 1984 we had seen super-fit Australians leaving exhausted Lions in their wake on runs such as this; now it was the turn of Lewis and Pearce to conduct a vain pursuit as Mike Gregory was roared home every step of the way by the exultant British crowd.

In the dying minutes, Hanley put Gill away for a last try, only to see his pass ruled forward by the referee. Great Britain were happy to settle for a 26–12 victory – the impossible dream. Mal was chaired off the field at the end of the match as the British fans crowded around in ecstasy, but he knew the debt he owed to his players. The unleashed flair of Ford, Gill and

Offiah; the rock-like solidity of Stephenson and Loughlin; the astonishing
work rate of David Hulme, with thirty-four tackles from stand-off; Andy
Gregory, producing a performance perhaps unequalled in Tests; Kevin
Ward, for this short time the undisputed king of world props, and the
unstinting Hugh Waddell; the unsung Roy Powell and the wholehearted
Paul Hulme, always at home in an alien position; and captain Hanley and
Mike Gregory, seventy punishing tackles between them – these were the
men whose performance against all the odds earned them a place in sporting
folklore.

Australia: Jack; Ettingshausen, O'Connor, Jackson, Currie; Lewis, Ster-
  ling; Bella, Conescu, Backo, Fullerton-Smith, Vautin, Pearce
  Substitutes: Belcher for Sterling after 33 minutes, Lindner for Fullerton-
  Smith after 66 minutes
  Scorers: tries – Lewis, Backo; goals – O'Connor (2)

Great Britain: Phil Ford (Bradford Northern); Gill (Wigan), Loughlin
  (St Helens), Stephenson (Leeds), Offiah (Widnes); David Hulme (Wid-
  nes), Andy Gregory (Wigan); Ward (Castleford), Paul Hulme (Widnes),
  Waddell (Oldham), Roy Powell (Leeds), Mike Gregory (Warrington), .
  Hanley (Wigan)
  Substitutes: Case (Wigan) for Waddell after 64 minutes; Wright (Widnes)
  not used
  Scorers: tries – Gill (2), Offiah, Phil Ford, Mike Gregory; goals –
  Loughlin (3)

Referee: F. Desplas (France)

The dressing-room was bedlam as everyone crowded in to share in the
success and to congratulate the boys. Mal was very quiet; he stood pale and
drawn with a suggestion of a satisfied smile as he drank his can of lager.
There was a brief halt to the proceedings, however, when Peter Frilingos,
the vitriolic Sydney reporter who had continually rubbished us and written
us off, entered the dressing-room. Mal fixed him with his laser-beam eyes
and invited him to leave, with or without assistance. Peter realised that
discretion was the better part of valour and beat a hasty retreat.

Reaction to our victory in the Australian media made satisfying reading.
The *Sydney Telegraph*'s headline was 'Mighty Lions Roar at Last!' Ray
Chesterton wrote, 'Tears flowed more freely than champagne in the Great
Britain dressing-room yesterday, with tough Rugby League players weeping
openly as one of the longest sieges in English sporting history was finally
lifted. A bits-and-pieces Great Britain side, held together with hope and
determination, finally achieved what former touring sides have been trying
to do for fourteen years in Australia – win a Test match.' John Hogan of the
Australian wrote, 'A makeshift and wounded team of British Lions not only

The final whistle blows on the third Test at Sydney in 1988 and (from left) Phil Larder, Mal Reilly, David Howes and Les Bettinson celebrate an historic triumph, achieved against all the odds with an injury-depleted team.

breathed life back into international Rugby League by beating Australia 26–12, but caused the biggest upset in the code's eighty-year history.'

The enormous boost that one victory gave to British Rugby League was incalculable, and its effect on the morale of everyone connected with the game was instantaneous. Tangible evidence of progress was there for all to see, and the people charged with the responsibility of promoting Rugby League were given a new surge of confidence and optimism. The victory marked a watershed at international level because it represented a psychological breakthrough for our players; the myth of Australian invincibility had finally been exposed. It didn't mean that success against future Australian sides was guaranteed – far from it. But it did mean that our players would no longer be in awe of them. They had demonstrated the skills, strength and will to compete on equal terms, whereas before their self-belief had been missing.

We flew from Sydney to Wellington via Christchurch to fulfil a contro-versial mid-week fixture against a district team coached by Howie Tamati. This was a fixture we had expected to have been cancelled months before, but a breakdown in communication had resulted in the International Board insisting that we fulfil the obligation. Since the match was only three days before the Test against New Zealand which decided a place in the World Cup final, we were less than pleased. We won the match 24–18 and did not pick up any more injuries, which was a relief. I could not help thinking that if only we had won the match against France in Avignon in 1986 instead of sharing the points then we would already have qualified for the World Cup final. That draw was to prove costly.

Preparation went well for the Test in Christchurch, and the only change we made from the third Test was Beardmore for Paul Hulme. The day of the match dawned with lashing rain aided and abetted by strong winds. Although the weather was the same for the Kiwis, we still felt anxious that playing conditions would be the deciding factor. When we got to the ground to find that a curtain-raiser was also taking place we could only shake our heads in disbelief.

Everyone was pretty tense because so much was riding on victory. Beating Australia had given all of us a great boost, but a World Cup final at Old Trafford, Manchester, would create fever-pitch enthusiasm for Rugby League in Britain, apart from the huge financial rewards it would generate. We didn't have to spell it out for the players; they knew what the consequences of defeat would be. In the third Test they had played for honour and pride; this game placed on them an increased burden of responsibility.

To a large extent New Zealand were fielding a new-look Test team with many of the old guard – the Sorensens, the Tamatis, Leuleuai and O'Hara – all gone. They also had a tough new coach called Tony Gordon who had inherited Graham Lowe's mantle and already had one Aussie scalp under his belt.

In the event the game was won and lost in the first half, with Great Britain playing into a fierce wind and driving rain, but still having by far the best of the exchanges. In the very first minute David Hulme broke from a scrum and, although he lost the ball in the tackle, Loughlin was on hand to scoop it up and score an opportunist try. But the big centre had left his kicking boots at home, and a string of missed penalties and the arrival of the mercurial Gary Freeman as a thirteenth-minute substitute handed the initiative to New Zealand.

After Peter Brown had landed a penalty, Freeman tore on to a masterly long ball from Shane Cooper to split Hulme and Stephenson and then beat Loughlin and Ford on his run to the line. Once again, Gregory had a try disallowed from a 'Wardy' move, and had injury added to his insult when he was flattened off the ball with the referee unsighted. Just before half-time, David Hulme crossed for a try from Hanley's well-timed pass, but just as it seemed that we would go in at the interval all square, Phil Ford knocked forward from the kick-off a metre from his own line. From the resulting scrum New Zealand worked the ball across the field, Sam Stewart stood up in the tackle and the irrepressible Freeman propped up to take the scoring pass.

The second half was a real war of attrition. New Zealand defended desperately as Great Britain's tactical plan, most especially their kicking game, disintegrated. The departure of Hanley with a cut eyebrow robbed the Lions of perhaps the one player who might have broken the game, and, although Loughlin clawed back 2 points with a penalty, New Zealand hung on to win 12–10. It was a very close-run thing.

New Zealand: Williams; Shane Horo, Bell, Kevin Iro, Mercer; Cooper, Friend; Brown, Wallace, Adrian Shelford, Graham, Stewart, Mark Horo
Substitutes: Freeman for Mark Horo after 13 minutes; Faimalo not used
Scorers: tries – Freeman (2); goals – Brown (2)

Great Britain: Phil Ford (Bradford Northern); Gill (Wigan), Loughlin (St Helens), Stephenson (Leeds), Offiah (Widnes); David Hulme (Widnes), Andy Gregory (Wigan); Ward (Castleford), Kevin Beardmore (Castleford), Waddell (Oldham), Roy Powell (Leeds), Mike Gregory (Warrington), Hanley (Wigan)
Substitutes: Paul Hulme (Widnes) for Hanley after 67 minutes; Wright (Widnes) not used
Scorers: tries – Loughlin, David Hulme; goal – Loughlin

Referee: M. Stone (Australia)

Mal and I made our way to a bleak dressing-room to console the dejected players, whose dreams of glory had been left behind in the mud of the Addington Showground. The Kiwis were cock-a-hoop. George Rainey, the New Zealand president, heralded the victory as, 'The greatest day the game has seen in its history. This puts us into the World Cup final, and the Kiwis have done what no team has ever done for us before today'. His euphoria was to be relatively short-lived, however, as the Kiwis crashed out 25–12 against Australia in front of a large home crowd at Eden Park in the World Cup final in October.

Although a fair amount of interest was generated in the final stages of the World Cup competition, it did not, in my view, justify a competition beginning on 7 July 1985 and concluding on 9 October 1988. Ten of the New Zealand players who won the first World Cup match against Australia in 1985 were no longer in contention for international selection by the time the final was played three years later. Of the original Great Britain side who began the campaign in October 1985, only Ellery Hanley survived to play in the final qualifying match against New Zealand in 1988; there were guys back in England who had retired by then. The International Board persuaded themselves that the competition had rivetting appeal to the public and media and immediately launched another marathon in 1989. This meant that yet another Rugby League World Cup would last almost as long as the Second World War. This is ridiculous: a more sensible arrangement must be worked out.

Our defeat against a combined Auckland team in the remaining match by 30–14 merely served to rub salt in our wounds. We had travelled to

The Leeds
utility forward
Roy Powell was
the model Lions
tourist, willing to
take the
field in every
match and
never giving
less than his
best. Although
not always
appreciated by
his own club,
Powell has
been a constant
feature in Mal
Reilly's
Test squads.

the impressive city of Auckland determined to win our final match, but I suspect many of the players were mentally already on the plane back home. Ten weeks on tour is a long time following a hard season of British football and a highly motivated and skilful Auckland team soon exposed our overall lack of enthusiasm for the match. It was the end of a tour that had taken up a large part of all our lives and the next day we were to set off for home.

On the way back Mal dropped off in Sydney with Hanley, Gill, Mike and Andy Gregory, and Ward to fulfil one last engagement, the Rest of the World match against Australia to celebrate Australia's bicentenary; Australia won 22–10. In fact Mal found himself a bit of a spare part when he got there as the team was coached by Graham Lowe, and he took the first opportunity to get a flight home: He was physically and emotionally drained; it was time to recharge his own batteries.

We all felt the same. Each of us had been engaged in an enterprise that we would remember for the rest of our lives – the camaraderie, friendship, and sharing of experiences had been something special. With the players we had set out to put British Rugby League on the international map, and although we never reached our goal, for one glorious moment we achieved the impossible dream and triumphed over Australia.

7

Paying the Price

Early in August 1988 the Rugby Football League council met to decide its future. Possible reform advocated earlier in the year by the chairman, Bob Ashby, had been in abeyance because of the Lions tour, and decisions due to be confirmed at the Annual General Meeting at the end of June had been postponed. A small sub-committee had been given the task of examining the reform proposals and recommending a strategy or course of action. Those proposals were:

1 That the term of office of the chairman should be extended to a minimum of three years;
2 That the secretary-general, David Oxley, should be upgraded to the position of chief executive;
3 That there should be a five-man board of directors;
4 That a new position of annually elected president should be created to fulfil official duties previously carried out by the chairman.

Bob Ashby called the council meeting to order and reiterated his reasons for advocating change. He emphasised that the proposals would benefit the game and speed up the bureaucratic machinery. He also said that his period of office had proved to him that one year was too short a period for any chairman to be effective.

Bob is an excellent chairman who has always fulfilled his duties very conscientiously. He loves to project the image of a simple Yorkshireman who calls a spade a spade, but in reality he is a successful businessman, an instinctive politician and a man who enjoys exercising power. This is not a criticism – quite the contrary; Bob's disarming 'hail-fellow-well-met' style is most effective in the hurly-burly of Rugby League politics and he uses it to good advantage. He believed that the game needed strong leadership and that he was capable of providing that. He received positive support and was unanimously elected to continue as chairman. David Oxley was duly upgraded to the position of chief executive.

The atmosphere was pretty heady that day, and attempts to seek clarification as to how the powers of the new board of directors would be exercised seemed to get swept away by enthusiastic reformers who considered such questions to be negative. The fact is that the Rugby Football League council was a federation of thirty-five (now thirty-six) separate states, each one governed and controlled differently. To suggest, therefore, that major policy decisions could be taken by a new executive without the majority approval of council was nonsense. The by-laws still existed, and changing any by-law needed a two-thirds majority whether there was a five-man board of directors or not. Such detail had yet to be worked out, it seemed. One or two reformers used words such as 'progressive thinking', and others nodded approvingly without really knowing what it meant.

There was a body of opinion that believed the new directors should be elected by council. Tom Smith of Widnes argued that the chairman should select his own board, and opinion moved strongly in favour of such a radical proposal. The vote was taken, and Bob was given a mandate to return to the next meeting with his recommendations for positions on the board, while council members were invited to declare their interest to David Oxley. It was *glasnost* and *perestroika* all rolled into one.

The council met within two weeks and the chairman recommended his board of directors. They were Maurice Lindsay of Wigan, a man who had formed a four-man board at Wigan in 1980 and, with his energy, enthusiasm and shrewd business acumen, made it the leading club in the country; Joe Seddon of St Helens, a popular, long-serving member of council and former chairman whose financial skills would be vital if the board was to control the cash flow; Harry Jepson of Leeds, a man steeped in the history and culture of the game who had fulfilled significant roles with Hunslet and Leeds, and led the colts league successfully for years; and Rodney Walker of Wakefield, a successful businessman who had come to Rugby League comparatively recently, but whose knowledge of the world of commerce and his association with television made him a useful recruit.

Bob's choices were well received and gained unanimous approval. I saw the new board as policy-makers, with time to focus on the key issues that the game needed to address: promotion, marketing, playing standards, ground safety, development and so on; and that they would present their ideas to council in the form of short- and long-term development plans. In reality, however, they were soon to find themselves bogged down with the immediacy of day-to-day decision-making, a problem they are still grappling with. Sniping soon began by council members who resented having some of their power eroded, and some clubs even voiced the opinion that members of the board should not have club positions because of vested interests. Some things never change.

Nevertheless the new board of directors set about their tasks with considerable energy and enthusiasm. The question of marketing and stand-ards of refereeing had been on the agenda for some time, and now the board were able to appoint full-time officers to take charge of these affairs. In the case of marketing, Mike Turner was engaged under the direction of Maurice Lindsay, while Fred Lindop, a recently retired referee, was appointed full-time controller of referees with a mandate to reform their whole training and development programme and to bring out a code of practice in keeping with the thrusting image of Rugby League as the family sport of the future. Other issues that had to be addressed were youth rugby, in partnership with BARLA in the newly formed District Development Associations; and ground safety legislation, which had swallowed up huge amounts of money before the board took on the task of developing a minimum standards policy for grounds which would force clubs to begin the process of rectifying years of decline and neglect.

For David Oxley, the decision taken by council to streamline its decision-making process meant a substantial loss of authority and control. His predecessor, Bill Fallowfield, had been able to establish a virtual autocracy, and this mantle had been passed to David. Now he would no longer be the ultimate authority at the Rugby Football League, as the chairman would take up centre-stage position. David Oxley, however, has been an outstanding administrator and spokesman for Rugby League. His diplomacy and status is widely recognised by other sports administrators, and his massive contribution to the development of the game is a matter of record. The award of an OBE in 1989 was a fitting tribute to his success as secretary-general and chief executive of the Rugby Football League.

I was appointed to be the first annually elected president. I was to have been chairman by rotation in 1988, but events had overtaken me. I was not sure how I was to fulfil the role of president, and to a large extent I had to invent it. There were times throughout the year when I, as president, and Bob, as chairman, seemed to be racing to get to the podium first – obviously a few operational details had been overlooked.

One of my first duties was to present specially designed commemorative medals to the players elected to Rugby League's new Hall of Fame, set up at the Bentley Arms, Rothwell. A five-man panel decided to be very selective and restrict the award to nine players, with the understanding that others could be added later; in fact the great Neil Fox was added in 1989. All the players selected are legends in the game: Billy Batten (1905–1927); Brian Bevan (1945–1964); Billy Boston (1953–1970); Alex Murphy (1956–1975); Jonty Parkin (1913–1932); Gus Risman (1929–1954); Albert Rosenfeld (1909–1924); Jim Sullivan (1921–1946); and Harold Wagstaff (1906–1925). The award ceremony was a very moving occasion as the great men or close relations stepped forward; today only Billy Boston, Gus Risman and Alex Murphy are still with us. The Hall of Fame contains photos, mementoes and memorabilia covering the history of Rugby League and is a mecca for rugby enthusiasts.

Part of the celebration included a special challenge match between Great

Britain and the Rest of the World on 29 October. This was contractually to be my final match as manager of Great Britain. We selected a strong team, relying heavily on players who had played in the third Test in Sydney. Injuries meant a few changes, but all the team bar David Plange had toured.

The match ended with a score of 30–28 in Great Britain's favour, which only proved that challenge matches tend to end up as exhibition matches despite all the hype and publicity. Mal was disappointed with our defensive work, but pleased to see Kevin Ward hold his Australian form and to welcome Shaun Edwards back to the fold.

It was during the preparations for the match against the Rest of the World that Mal Reilly, Phil Larder and myself discussed the future. I specifically put it to Mal that his continuation as coach was essential; but Mal was now coaching Leeds, and the tradition was that the national coach should not have a club connection. The press were already speculating about the future, and although Mal was not prepared to make a statement, I was. I took the opportunity during the press conference at the end of the match against the Rest of the World to say, 'As far as I'm concerned, it's not even a matter of debate. Mal Reilly should continue to be the Great Britain coach, and if you don't believe me ask the players. Why, after all that's been achieved, jeopardise everything by a bit of bureaucratic red tape?'

I sought a meeting with Bob Ashby to seek some assurances about the future and to press for the reappointment of Mal Reilly. The meeting opened with some strong exchanges, as the chairman felt that I had had too much too say about the position of the Great Britain coach. Bob declared that any decisions as to the future would be taken by himself and the board. I defended my corner vigorously, and emphasised the reasons why Mal Reilly, and by extension Phil Larder and myself, should continue as a team. Bob was willing to concede most of the points I was making, but I was thrown by one question he put to me which was to re-appear twelve months later: 'Do we need a manager on future tours?' I left the meeting not entirely sure of the chairman's next move, although Bob went on to negotiate a new contract with Mal Reilly and in due course announced that the Great Britain management team that had functioned on the 1988 tour would continue until the visit of the Kiwis in autumn 1989.

In preparation for the 1989 Kiwi series we had two matches against France in which to experiment and blood new talent. The first match was on 21 January 1989 at Central Park, Wigan, where injury to Steve Hampson enabled us to introduce an exciting new full-back from Widnes called Alan Tait. Alan's father was a Scot who had played for Workington before returning to Scotland, and Alan was already a full Scottish Rugby Union international when Doug Laughton signed him for Widnes and successfully converted him from centre to full-back. Injuries to Schofield and Stephenson provided Peter Williams of Salford, the former England Rugby Union stand-off, with his chance to become a dual international. In addition, Joe Lydon was persuaded to return to the fold, although his bitterness over missing the 1988 tour was pretty deep-rooted. Unfortunately Des Drummond resisted similar attempts, and maintained his vow never to play for his country again.

Great Britain found it very difficult to work up any head of steam at Wigan, and were constantly upstaged by the good work of the French forwards, Buttignol, Verdes and Moliner, and their half-backs, Palisses and Dumas, who inspired much entertaining football. Although Great Britain won 26–10, the only significant highlight of their performance was the exciting début of Alan Tait, who was a constant threat in attack and fully deserved his man-of-the-match award. Given the tradition of the French for pulling off shocks on their own home ground, there were definite alarm bells for Mal Reilly as he looked ahead to the return match in Avignon.

Great Britain: Tait (Widnes); Phil Ford (Leeds), Loughlin (St Helens), Lydon (Wigan), Offiah (Widnes); Edwards (Wigan), Andy Gregory (Wigan); Ward (Castleford), Kevin Beardmore (Castleford), Waddell (Leeds), Mike Gregory (Warrington), Roy Powell (Leeds), Hanley (Wigan)
Substitutes: Eyres (Widnes) for Roy Powell after 62 minutes, Williams (Salford) for Offiah after 66 minutes
Scorers: tries – Edwards, Hanley, Phil Ford, Offiah, Lydon; goals – Loughlin (3)

France: Fraisse; Ratier, Delaunay, Eric Vergniol, Criottier; Palisses, Dumas; Rabot, Valero, Aillères, Buttignol, Verdes, Moliner
Substitutes: Tisseyre for Rabot after 62 minutes, Rocci for Palisses after 69 minutes
Scorers: tries – Moliner, Dumas; goal – Fraisse

Referee: G. McCallum (Australia)

For the return match Peter Williams stepped up from the bench for the injured Loughlin, and Lee Crooks was given the opportunity to reclaim his Test place at the expense of Hugh Waddell. The match was memorable because it was the fiftieth Test between the two countries. Mal's fears proved groundless as we put on a superb display of attacking rugby to win by a margin of 30–8. Hanley was in irresistible form as Great Britain shot into a 10-point lead, and the French were overwhelmed. Lee Crooks gave notice that he was back in business with an outstanding game in the front row alongside Kevin Ward. It was the sort of game we had hoped for from Lee in Australia; better late than never.

France: Frison; Ratier, Delaunay, Eric Vergniol, Fraisse; Palisses, Dumas; Rabot, Valero, Aillères, Buttignol, Verdes, Moliner
Substitutes: Rocci for Dumas after 46 minutes, Tisseyre for Rabot after 61 minutes
Scorers: tries – Dumas, Ratier

Great Britain: Tait (Widnes); Phil Ford (Leeds), Williams (Salford), Lydon (Wigan), Offiah (Widnes); Edwards (Wigan), Andy Gregory (Wigan); Ward (Castleford), Kevin Beardmore (Castleford), Crooks (Leeds), Mike Gregory (Warrington), Roy Powell (Leeds), Hanley (Wigan)
Substitutes: England (Castleford) for Roy Powell after 62 minutes, Hampson (Wigan) for Phil Ford after 69 minutes
Scorers: tries – Phil Ford (2), Edwards, Tait, Hanley, Williams; goals – Lydon (3)

Referee: G. McCallum (Australia)

Castleford hooker Kevin Beardmore drives the ball into the French defence in January 1988, supported by Hugh Waddell (left) and Widnes's Richard Eyres, making his Test début as a substitute.

Mal, Phil and I discussed the close season and decided not to institute a programme of international training during the summer months, but to arrange for a battery of tests at Lilleshall before the end of the season. With a grant from the Sports Council we had negotiated a programme of tests administered by John Brewer of Loughborough University. The tests were more scientific than had been used previously, and each player was presented with a detailed dossier indicating his fitness levels with targets and goals for the future. The players would be retested at the beginning of the 1989–90 season. It was a fair indication of progress that we felt confident enough to delegate responsibility to individual players, and was the outcome of the programme of player education.

By 1989 Great Britain had not won a Test series against New Zealand on home soil since 1965, and although I was confident that we were about to put the record straight I also knew that victory was not going to come easily. We went into the series with new sponsors, British Coal, who saw that their slogan 'The new face of British Coal' matched up well with the rejuvenation of the British Lions as a force in international Rugby League. They brought along a new mascot, too: George, a seven-foot silver miner, who even put big Roy Powell in the shade! They were ideal sponsors to work with, and the sport of Rugby League was much the healthier for their association.

Mal, Phil and I decided to bring the squad into camp for the full week before the first Test at Old Trafford. I had some reservations about this and expressed the view that we should meet on the Monday afternoon for daylight training, but that the players should then return home until the Wednesday. This, I believed, would reduce the boredom factor but still leave enough time to bring the players to a peak. In the end we agreed on a compromise which was to spend the first half of the week at Lilleshall, before travelling up to the traditional Great Britain camp at Shaw Hill, where there would be a change of emphasis to shorter practice sessions with plenty of opportunity for rest.

The Kiwis were captained by Hugh McGahan and coached by Tony 'Tank' Gordon. Although their squad included several familiar faces it was also clear that they were undergoing a process of change as older players were being replaced by up-and-coming youngsters. Informed opinion found it difficult to assess the strengths of the Kiwis, as their form in the opening matches was far from convincing. By the time they approached the first Test, however, they had managed to win four matches but had lost to St Helens and Wigan.

We had problems of our own, which started with Ellery Hanley returning from his summer stint in Australia having sustained damage to his groin and stomach muscles. When it was announced that surgery was necessary and that he would not resume playing until the New Year, our confidence was somewhat dented; losing Ellery was a considerable blow. We were beginning to feel decidedly shaky, however, when Andy Gregory and Garry Schofield sustained serious leg injuries in the annual clash between Lancashire and Yorkshire. To add to our woes Joe Lydon was carrying a troublesome thigh strain and Kevin Ward had an ankle injury. Denis Betts, the promising Wigan second-rower who had been pencilled into the squad, also suffered a severe hamstring strain.

Two weeks before the first British Coal Test we had decided that David Hulme and Shaun Edwards would be our half-back pairing. We then began to have our hopes raised that Andy Gregory would recover, especially when he decided to prove his fitness by playing for Wigan the week before the Test match. When the players settled in at Lilleshall, the first question we had to address was whether Andy was fit to play. Although he lacked match fitness his torn hamstring appeared to have recovered, as he had played most of the game for Wigan at the weekend. On top of that, he was keen to play. In the end we came down in Andy's favour and voted to go into the match with him as scrum-half. He was regarded as a central figure in our game plan, and we were confident that he would provide the necessary platform for victory.

Andy Gegory's position at half-back for the first Kiwi Test in 1989 was the matter of considerable debate as he battled his way back from injury. In the end, his performance showed that he was not match fit, and he was omitted from the rest of the series.

The next question was that of stand-off: were we to go for the Wigan pairing of Gregory and Edwards, or the pairing of Gregory and Hulme who had served us well on tour? Both Edwards and Hulme were on top form, and Hulme in particular had excelled in the World Club Challenge match between Widnes and Canberra Raiders earlier in October. Slowly but surely opinion began to move in favour of Hulme on the basis of his aggressive defence. Edwards's attacking skills were not in question, but we began to persuade ourselves that he and Gregory as a combination had some potential weakness in defence. Mal believed that if we started solidly with Hulme closing down the middle of the field, Edwards could be brought on later as a tactical ploy.

The question of defence came up when we discussed the centre pairing. Andy Currier had returned from a sensational summer spell with Balmain that had culminated in a place in the Grand Final. He had grabbed headlines every week in Australia with his powerful running and accurate goal-kicking, but Mal and Phil had serious reservations about his shirt-grabbing tackling technique, which we had seen at first hand on the 1988 tour. I argued that Andy's spell in Australia must have improved his defence and that his new-found confidence would make him an explosive centre at Test level. He and Paul Loughlin would give us a formidable combination of size, strength and power. The alternative now that Joe Lydon had been ruled out was to blood Paul Newlove, the talented teenager from Featherstone, which was perhaps an unnecessary gamble.

Before Andy Gregory came back into contention we had agreed that Mike Gregory, already captain of Warrington, was the ideal replacement captain for Ellery Hanley. Mike was experienced and popular with the players, although on the 1988 tour Andy Gregory had been vice-captain and I knew he had an unfulfilled ambition to captain his country. In the end we elected to stay with our original choice of Mike Gregory.

I suggested to Mal that he would need to let Shaun Edwards know before the team was announced that he was to start as substitute. I knew that Shaun would find this decision very hard to cope with because he was desperate to establish himself as a world-class stand-off. As the players gathered for the first training session I observed Mal and Shaun together. I could tell from their expressions that neither was enjoying the conversation, and Shaun's face registered the hurt he was feeling. When Mal announced his team and appointed Mike Gregory captain, I was also sensitive to Andy's disappointment although he was the first to congratulate Mike. Mal spoke to Andy privately as there was great mutual respect between them; Andy accepted Mal's reasoning, but it didn't ease the disappointment.

By Wednesday several of the players were complaining of having heavy legs and feeling tired. The coaches immediately took steps to modify the training programme, but six training sessions each of two hours duration was a change of routine for most of the players, and they were having to adjust more than we had anticipated. Training at Shaw Hill went well, but there was still something missing that the coaches could not pin down; complacency, perhaps, a lack of tension or an over-familiarity with the old routine. Whatever it was, we did not lose any sleep over it and were confident of victory.

In the event, our selectorial decisions and our carefully planned preparations all blew up in our faces. New Zealand played with an eagerness and determination that Great Britain just could not match, and in Gary Freeman they had the dominant individual, just as he had been in Auckland in 1988. Sniping, prompting and cajoling, Freeman brought the best out of his powerful pack and provided the ideal link for his free-running backs. The British six had no response; Kelvin Skerrett made a useful début, but the recalled David Hobbs could never work his kicking game to good effect. New Zealand were 16–6 up at half-time with tries by forwards Goulding and McGahan and Kelly Shelford, after Kevin Iro had decimated Great Britain's defence on the end of Freeman's pass. David Hulme's break led to Phil Ford's try, but it was a temporary inconvenience for the Kiwis.

With Andy Gregory anonymous and clearly suffering, and Currier missing tackles even when under no pressure, the way was clear for Shaun Edwards to breathe life back into Great Britain. His introduction early in the second half followed a superb score by Freeman, made by Duane Mann's incursion into a breathtaking move, but Edwards was soon involved in a liaison with Hulme that saw Ford and Offiah make ground before Tait scored in the corner. Then Offiah, having an extraordinary duel with Kevin Iro, twisted away from the acting half-back position in his own 22, handed off Iro and turned Mercer inside out on a brilliant weaving run to the line. It was Iro who had the last laugh, however, taking a blind-side ball from Freeman and going through Offiah, as well as Goodway and Hobbs, for the final score to win the match for New Zealand by 24–16.

The Widnes centre Andy Currier lasted only fifty-five minutes of his Test début against New Zealand in 1989 before his defensive deficiencies became a liability. It had been hoped that a summer in Australia would have added strength in this department to his undoubted running ability.

Great Britain: Tait (Widnes); Phil Ford (Leeds), Currier (Widnes), Loughlin (St Helens), Offiah (Widnes); David Hulme (Widnes), Andy Gregory (Wigan); Skerrett (Bradford Northern), Kevin Beardmore (Castleford), Hobbs (Bradford Northern), Goodway (Wigan), Platt (Wigan), Mike Gregory (Warrington)
Substitutes: Edwards (Wigan) for Currier after 55 minutes, Newlove (Featherstone Rovers) for Phil Ford after 75 minutes; Roy Powell (Leeds) and Paul Hulme (Widnes) not used
Scorers: tries – Phil Ford, Tait, Offiah; goals – Loughlin (2)

New Zealand: Williams; Kevin Iro, Bell, Sherlock, Mercer; Kelly Shelford, Freeman; Goulding, Duane Mann, Todd, Kurt Sorensen, Stewart, McGahan

Substitutes: Kemp for Williams after 77 minutes; Bancroft, Kuiti and Leota not used

Scorers: tries – Goulding, McGahan, Kelly Shelford, Freeman, Kevin Iro; goals – Sherlock (2)

When the chips were down Great Britain had failed, and there were no acceptable excuses. Andy Gregory summed it up when he said to Mal, 'That's the worst game I've ever played in my life.' Andy was speaking from the heart, but not all had the guts to say it. The players were deeply ashamed and knew that they had let themselves, Great Britain and Mal Reilly down. Next door we could hear the Kiwis singing and shouting as they celebrated a victory that no one except themselves had predicted.

Later, in the Old Trafford board-room Tom Mitchell, a senior member of the Rugby Football League council and an elder statesman in the game, quizzed me as to our selection policy. He said that he was expressing the views of senior officials and 'others' who had doubted the wisdom of playing Currier and Ford, believed that we were wrong not to start with Edwards and thought we had gambled unwisely on Gregory's fitness. I was quite happy to comment on these views to Tom, but when I learned later that David Oxley had not only expressed the same opinions to the New Zealand press, but had gone on to say that in future the board would probably have a greater say in selection, I knew that our credibility had diminished. I was tempted to challenge David on the matter, but I knew that he tended to work himself into a state of anxiety at international matches even when we won, so I decided to let it pass.

The coaches and I met at Rugby Football League HQ on the Monday before the second British Coal Test to analyse the events of the disastrous first Test and select a new team. As we sat down to carry out the post mortem we were joined by David Oxley who asked if he could sit in on the discussion. Mal and I exchanged glances, but we had nothing to hide and he was the chief executive after all. I decided that he could sit in, but that he would have no part in the proceedings. Later I reflected on David's presence but could only speculate as to his motives: was he there on his own initiative, or had the chairman suggested it?

The first part of the meeting centred on an analysis of the overall team performance. The error count had catapulted to forty, which was as bad as it could possibly have been. We had to accept that training twice a day prior to the match had possibly depleted stores of energy in some players. Training twice a day on tour is normal, but then the player tolerance and fitness levels rise accordingly. Introducing such a regime one week before a Test could have been counter-productive.

The most critical decision was, again, whether to pair Gregory and Edwards or Hulme and Edwards. Like it or not, Andy Gregory had not been able to control the game as we had hoped, and his lack of match fitness coupled with a poor performance by the pack had left him exposed. The final decision to drop Andy was one that Mal had difficulty in coming to terms with. He had built up a strong bond with Andy during his period as coach, and to abandon him after one poor game seemed to him be grossly unfair and against our basic principles. However, Mal was prepared to face up to the fact that Andy was not match fit and one week wasn't going to rectify that. The alternative, David Hulme, would be able to put a tighter rein on Freeman who had cut us to shreds. The decision was made and Mal had the difficult task of telling Andy whose pride, he knew, would be hurt.

Phil Ford, who had not enjoyed one of his most confident games on the wing, was also put under the microscope but survived the examination. Currier was replaced by Paul Newlove (a gamble which we could now justify), and Andy Platt was moved up to replace Hobbs in the front row. The final change was to include tough-tackling Paul Hulme in the second row. The team met on the Wednesday morning, which gave us three days to complete the necessary transformation.

The players were resolved to put the record straight, but as Andy Goodway used to remind them at regular intervals, 'Talk's cheap'. Mike Gregory was finding the transfer from player to captain quite demanding. Mike is an extrovert and gregarious by nature. On tour he had been a key member of the 'social set' and was an outstanding tourist; now he was having to adjust his role, and Mal felt he should be assertive and rein in one or two who seemed to be stretching the rules. You don't become a Great Britain captain overnight, and being captain means on and off the field. Mike's commitment and strong personality, however, made him a quick learner.

On the morning before the second British Coal Test I had to go into work to clear my in-tray. When I returned at lunch-time Mal and Phil's faces said it all. Alan Tait had pulled a hamstring in the final training session and Kevin Beardmore's shoulder was still sensitive to pain. We quickly arranged to bring Steve Hampson into camp and move Paul Hulme to hooker, allowing Roy Powell to play in the second row. In some ways Roy Powell has not fulfilled his true potential, but as a man to be relied on in a crisis there is no one better. He is a friendly man, warm-hearted and a true professional. Nature failed to give him a mean streak, but then we are born as human beings, not as Rugby League players.

The final team meeting was held on the Friday evening after dinner. Normally team meetings are rather quiet affairs but this one was different. Mal asked if anyone was missing. One of the players named Andy Gregory and Andy Currier, both of whom had been dropped from the first Test. Mal's reaction was swift and decisive. He turned on the players, and said, 'If you think you can beat New Zealand with this complacent attitude, you can think again. As a matter of fact your attitude stank in the first Test and we paid the penalty. Now it seems that some of you are still labouring under the misapprehension that you only have to turn up to win. If you think that, then think again. I am just about ready to kick some ass, and it's going to be sooner rather than later'. The air was electric. No one dared catch Mal's eye but the effect was dramatic; he had stopped the rot.

The second British Coal Test at Elland Road, Leeds, on 28 October began in sensational style. Having fielded a high ball behind the goal-line Steve Hampson found himself hampered by Gary Freeman as he attempted to get the ball to the 22-metre line for a quick restart. Hampson took the law into his own hands and disposed of Freeman with a head butt; Greg McCallum, the referee, immediately dismissed him from the field of play. It was a personal tragedy for Steve and a monumental disaster for Great Britain.

Yet far from unnerving Hampson's team-mates, his dismissal had the effect of redoubling their determination. The reshuffle of the twelve remaining men took Loughlin to full-back and Andy Goodway out of the pack and into the centre. There he had the match of his life, snuffing out the threat of his Wigan club-mate, Kevin Iro, and showing a real threequarter's opportunism to snatch two vital tries. Yet it was Edwards, reassuming what he believed to be his rightful place in the side, who was the prime mover in Great Britain's success. He scored the first try himself,

The moment in the second Kiwi Test of 1989 when referee McCallum sent off Great Britain full-back Steve Hampson for butting Gary Freeman as he impeded his efforts to restart the game. Hampson's misery was compounded when he was sent off again the following day in a league match.

going in at the corner following a delightful five-man move, and made the second for Offiah by linking up with Skerrett's storming run, to give his team a 12–0 half-time lead.

In the second half it was Edwards again, sending Goodway in for the first of his tries and clocking up an astonishing number of tackles alongside his undermanned forwards and half-back partner, David Hulme. Hulme did such a good job on Freeman that the Kiwi was reduced to niggling and whingeing and even the sin bin, his influence on the game negated. That being the case, New Zealand never got out of first gear and spread the ball only once, for Mercer to outstrip the defence and give the scoring pass inside to McGahan. But that was after Goodway had charged down Williams's kick for Great Britain's final try. A victory margin of 26–6 reflected how emphatically the twelve men had dominated the game.

Andy Goodway, moved to the centre after Hampson's dismissal in the second Kiwi Test of 1989, dominated the exchanges out wide and scored two great opportunist's tries.

Great Britain: Hampson (Wigan); Phil Ford (Leeds), Newlove (Featherstone Rovers), Loughlin (St Helens), Offiah (Widnes); Edwards (Wigan), David Hulme (Widnes); Skerrett (Bradford Northern), Paul Hulme (Widnes), Platt (Wigan), Goodway (Wigan), Roy Powell (Leeds), Mike Gregory (Warrington)
Substitutes: Hobbs (Bradford Northern) for Skerrett after 65 minutes, Fox (Featherstone Rovers) for David Hulme after 74 minutes; Daryl Powell (Sheffield Eagles) and England (Castleford) not used
Scorers: tries – Goodway (2), Edwards, Offiah; goals – Loughlin (5)

New Zealand: Williams; Kevin Iro, Bell, Sherlock, Mercer; Kelly Shelford, Freeman; Adrian Shelford, Duane Mann, Todd, Kurt Sorensen, Stewart, McGahan

Substitutes: Faimalo for Adrian Shelford after 37 minutes, Kemp for Sherlock after 65 minutes; Bancroft and Leota not used

Scorers: try – McGahan; goal – Sherlock

Referee: G. McCallum (Australia)

Informed opinion agreed that it had been one of the great Test victories in the face of adversity, and the press were ecstatic. John Robinson wrote in the *Rugby Leaguer*: 'Great Britain, reaping the benefit of Mal Reilly's seven-day cure for teams of nervous disposition, did a marvellous job in levelling the British Coal Test series. Their transformation from chumps to champs in just a week was nothing less than amazing.'

We only needed to make one change for the final British Coal Test, and that was to reinstate Alan Tait at full-back. We did have a scare over David Hulme who had been battling with a damaged ankle for several weeks and needed specialist reassurance that he would not damage it further by playing.

The build-up for the deciding Test at Central Park, Wigan, reminded me of the third Test at Elland Road in 1985 when we had similarly needed victory over the Kiwis to clinch the series. Then we had been confident of success, but the match was a war of attrition and ended as a draw. Mal and I knew that the Kiwis were not about to roll over as they, too, had fierce pride and patriotic fervour which would make them highly competitive and dangerous. They were ashamed of their performance in the second Test and were determined to wipe out its memory by humiliating us in our home soil. Usually the last minutes before leaving the dressing-room are quiet, but, as in 1985, the Kiwis performed their *haka* in a blatant attempt to unnerve us. Our players gritted their teeth as the primitive tribal sounds washed over them. 'It's out on the pitch that counts,' said Mal. 'Remember: play to the game plan – keep your discipline – no backward steps. Our time has come.'

It was never going to be a classic game of Rugby League, given what was at stake and the wet, muddy conditions. But it was never less than exciting, particularly when Shaun Edwards raced through a gap early on to make a simple try for Offiah, who had tracked him all the way. Offiah almost grabbed a second in a frantic kick-and-chase from a loose ball, before Great Britain scored a try that would have been remarkable in any conditions, let alone these treacherous ones. Over seventy metres the ball went through eight pairs of hands, the crucial incursion being that of the teenager Newlove, before Tait rounded the cover defence for a spectacular try in the corner. Despite missing several shots at goal, Great Britain could feel that a 10–0 lead was emphatic.

Before half-time, however, Sam Stewart broke from acting half-back and unloaded in the tackle to Kelly Shelford, who side-stepped his way over by the posts. He converted his own try to make the interval score 10–6. New Zealand were encouraged by this, and after the break it took a superb last-ditch tackle by Tait to deny Faimalo the equalising score. Freeman then ignored the unmarked Mercer on his outside to spurn a further chance, and Mercer himself had a try disallowed by referee McCallum. Any grievance the Kiwis may have felt at this, however, was cancelled out by McCallum's decision not to award a penalty try after Phil Ford had been crudely hauled down by Dean Bell as they raced neck and neck after David Hulme's kick. In the end it was a colossal defensive effort by Great Britain, led by Mike Gregory, the Hulmes and Offiah, whose man-of-the-match award was perhaps uncharacteristically hard won, that brought the Lions their victory and a famous British Coal series win.

Widnes full-back Alan Tait completed a successful conversion from Rugby Union when he scored tries in both the first and third Kiwi Tests of 1989, the latter giving Great Britain victory in the series.

Great Britain: Tait (Widnes); Phil Ford (Leeds), Newlove (Featherstone Rovers), Loughlin (St Helens), Offiah (Widnes); Edwards (Wigan), David Hulme (Widnes); Skerrett (Bradford Northern), Paul Hulme (Widnes), Platt (Wigan), Goodway (Wigan), Roy Powell (Leeds), Mike Gregory (Warrington)
Substitutes: Lydon (Wigan) for Newlove after 32 minutes, England (Castleford) for Skerrett after 52 minutes; Fox (Featherstone Rovers) and Hobbs (Bradford Northern) not used
Scorers: tries – Offiah, Tait; goal – Loughlin

New Zealand: Kemp; Kevin Iro, Bell, Williams, Mercer; Kelly Shelford, Freeman; Todd, Duane Mann, Faimalo, Kurt Sorensen, Stewart, McGahan
Substitutes: Leota for Faimalo after 52 minutes, Clark for Kelly Shelford after 61 minutes; Sherlock and Kuiti not used
Scorers: try – Kelly Shelford; goal – Kelly Shelford

Referee: G. McCallum (Australia)

Mike Gregory raised the British Coal Trophy above his head and the crowd roared. As John Huxley wrote in the *Rugby Leaguer*, paraphrasing the Duke of Wellington at Waterloo, 'It was a damn close-run thing', but the players were now in the record book and another giant stride had been taken in our quest for world supremacy in Rugby League. France, Papua New Guinea and New Zealand had all been defeated; now remained the final challenge – Australia. But that was twelve months away, and twelve months in sport is a lifetime.

At British Coal's post-match reception Mal, Phil and I were finally able to relax and join in the celebrations. For several weeks we had been wound up like coiled springs; yet now that the goal had been achieved there was a slight feeling of anti-climax. Perhaps that was inevitable because in the end the glory belonged to the players. They had shown character and determination in withstanding the final Kiwi assault and more than deserved their success.

During the evening I sought out David Oxley to suggest that Mal's position as coach for the next tour and the subsequent series against Australia in autumn 1990 should be confirmed as soon as possible. I pointed out that Mal had been under a lot of pressure, and it was possible that the thought of a ten-week tour might have lost some of its appeal. David reassured me that there would be no delay and that speculation in the press about Mal's future after our defeat in the first Test was entirely unwarranted, as he and the board recognised all that had been achieved in recent years.

Two weeks later Mal and I met the board of directors at Headingley to present our reports. I reviewed our preparation and the significant features of the Test series, pinpointing areas where we had succeeded and others where we had been less successful. Bob Ashby, the chairman, then invited Mal to comment, but prefaced his remarks with a curious phrase: 'I won't call you coach, Malcolm, because in my eyes you're more of a manager.' Mal was actually embarrassed by this and quickly emphasised that he did not see it that way, but that the two roles were quite separate but complementary.

The discussion moved to the forthcoming tour of Papua New Guinea and New Zealand, and reports of key players stating that they did not intend to tour, but would rather play in Australia or enjoy a well-earned rest. The combined tour had not got the appeal of Australia and, in any case, ten weeks away from home produces its own stresses and strains. To ask players to do it every two years places an unfair burden on families. I had every sympathy with the likes of David Hulme, who had given everything in the 1988 and 1989 Test series, when he said that he preferred to take his wife and baby with him to Australia where he could realise his ambitions to play in the Sydney competition and cash in on his ability.

I urged the board to renegotiate the tour, recommending that if we went to New Zealand first we could play the Test matches at the beginning of the tour and then release our top players from the obligation to travel to Papua New Guinea; we would then have the opportunity to replace them in PNG with up-and-coming youngsters. I was concerned lest we take punitive action against players refusing to tour which would totally wreck our chances against Australia in the autumn; I could visualise a situation where threats of suspension would lead to confrontation if we weren't careful. The board shared my concern, but pointed out that host countries had the major say in the fixture format of a tour, as we did when we were the hosts, and that it would not be possible to reverse decisions already taken. Bob Ashby did say, however, that he intended to speak to Ken Arthurson, the president of the ARL, to encourage him not to accept the registrations of British players for Sydney teams if they had refused to tour – a black-list, in other words.

The meeting was frank and positive, and I felt confident that the board saw Mal and myself as a successful partnership. Bob Ashby thanked us and ended by saying that because of a full agenda they would discuss the Great Britain management at the next meeting. Looking back I now realise that it was a delaying strategy; if Bob had chosen to he could have had us reappointed there and then. But then hindsight has always been better than foresight. The board of directors met two weeks later to consider the structure of international management. I was not present and can only record subsequent events in a totally personal and subjective interpretation.

On the day of the meeting I received several 'phone calls from members of the press shortly after 5:00 p.m. They informed me that a rather odd statement had emanated from Rugby Football League HQ, to the effect that there would be no official announcement until further consultation had taken place. I was invited to comment and with total naivety suggested that they were probably sorting out a few details of Malcolm's contract. As the press were confident that I would be reappointed in the natural course of events they accepted my explanation as being the only logical one.

Being manager of Great Britain was the crowning point of my career in a sport that had been a central focus of my life. It was a task I relished and took pride in, and it was a job without salary. During my period of office I had built up a wealth of experience and knowledge which I assumed would be put to good use in 1990 when we had to play ten Test matches in eight months. There had been no official indication that I would not be asked to continue. My frame of mind, therefore, when I received a 'phone call from Bob Ashby at 7:00 p.m., was not quite as it had been in

1985 when, in competition with several others, I had anxiously entered the council chamber not knowing whether I had been elected manager. Four years on no other nominations had been sought, no other job specification had been published, there were no other challengers for the position and I was the experienced and proven manager. I was about to be knocked off my pedestal.

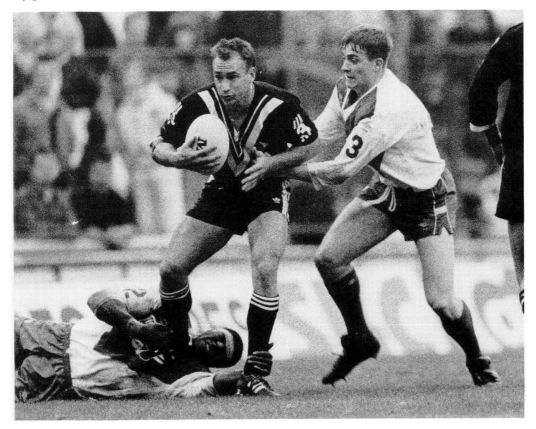

Bob's words were: 'Hello Les! I'm sorry, I've got some bad news for you. At the last minute another hat came into the ring – up to then it was a rubber-stamping job, but one of the board recommended Maurice Lindsay and it seemed he was ideally suited to the position of tour director. He was asked to leave the room and we took a vote. I'm sorry to be the bearer of bad news, Les.'

To say I was stunned would be the understatement of the year. I muttered 'Well, that's it, then,' and the 'phone call was over. Was that really it? Five years' work, and suddenly I was deposed without the opportunity to defend my position. The irony of it was, I had arranged an interview with my boss for the following day to request ten weeks' leave of absence without pay.

I sat for several hours and brooded over the injustice and the manner in which the proceedings had been conducted. It seemed that a new job specification had been agreed in my absence. When I was first appointed

Paul Newlove (right) helps Roy Powell to tackle New Zealand's Dean Bell. Omitted from the first Test team because of his inexperience, Newlove became Great Britain's youngest ever international when he came on as a substitute.

to the position of manager, Great Britain's stock was at rock bottom and I had had to write my own job specification. I decided what needed to be done and, in partnership with the coaches, got on with it. By 1989 I knew a great deal about being manager of Great Britain, and yet overnight it seemed I no longer fitted the role. To this day no new job specification has appeared in print, although Bob Ashby is quoted as saying, 'At first, we thought that Les would have to take on extra responsibility on the business side, but then we took the view that his background was purely in handling the playing side and we wondered if he was an administrator.'

Having been a senior administrator for twenty years, I found Bob's observation incomprehensible. Of course, I had had an outstanding business manager, David Howes, with me on tour in 1988. My role as manager was to oversee and co-ordinate the work of the business, playing, coaching and medical staff – that's what I thought managing meant. The real essence of the job is the trust, the bond that develops between committed professionals. That is something not easily achieved and yet, on the eve of the most critical period of Great Britain's international programme, in the knowledge that they had an area under their charge that was efficient, effective and stable, the board nevertheless chose to dismantle it in one short meeting and appoint one of their own colleagues.

Perhaps it was the area of public relations that the board had taken for granted, overlooking the fact that I represented the stability and integrity essential if you are to gain public confidence and trust. There was now the general perception that at international level there was a discernible strategy, a coaching development plan and clear evidence of progress. That's not to say that everything in the garden was rosy or that we were above criticism, but the game of Rugby League was again something to be proud of and the manager and coaches in charge of its international affairs knew what they were doing. A lot of hard work had been put into projecting a positive image to the players and to the public – one of openness, honesty, and commitment.

All the next day the telephone rang as word passed among the press corps like wildfire. All of them sympathised, thanked me for my work and wished me well. David Burke, a freelance writer, rang me to seek a quote, and it seemed apt to liken it to Julius Caesar's assassination on the steps of the senate – there were definite parallels! I went on to say that, 'I question whether it's constitutional; it's certainly of doubtful morality and smacks of nepotism'. Normally I would have been more circumspect in my response, but I decided that perhaps my diplomacy had been synonymous with weakness in the eyes of some. Although I had nothing personal against Maurice Lindsay, a very able and enlightened administrator, I was appalled at the inept and incompetent way my position had been handled – I was angry!

If I thought that my sacking would take up two or three lines in the newspapers I had another think coming; reaction to the news became a major talking point. John Huxley, editor of the *Rugby Leaguer*, wrote: 'The decision to remove Les Bettinson as Great Britain team manager was bad enough. Its delivery was diabolical! Had a player behaved that badly or a club official stepped that far out of line, they would have been charged with bringing the game into disrepute. The fact of the matter is that the board of directors are beyond the reach of that particular charge, but it still does not remove the smell of the whole proceedings. I don't believe there would be too many club coaches or managers who would change a winning team, and I don't understand why a switch of personnel was necessary in any case. What Maurice Lindsay may achieve or what he brings into the job doesn't really enter into it. There are so many questions left unanswered. How long is Mr Lindsay's appointment to last? Does he have a contract? Why wasn't the job advertised or at least offered to a wider range of candidates?'

Under the headline BETTINSON BLUNDER, John Robinson wrote:

'Les Bettinson has left a tough act for Maurice Lindsay to follow as Great Britain manager. He was more than just a supportive friend to coaches Maurice Bamford and Malcolm Reilly. In Britain's dark hours – and there were a few of those in his time – he had a warming gift for seeing light at the end of the tunnel. Many have been encouraged by his optimism and constructive advice. Day or night, he was available to be quoted by the press no matter how tricky the question. He countered criticism with diplomacy, never once slamming down the phone as some others might have. There were occasions when his opinions were forceful, but opponents were always afforded the right to disagree. What, then, it should be asked, did he do wrong to be so unceremoniously dumped from the job? The answer is NOTHING. Bettinson has not had the benefit of an explanation, other than that Maurice Lindsay was seen as the 'best man for the job'. There can be no doubting that, as a shrewd businessman and visionary, the Wigan chairman is second to none. It is reasonably safe to assume, however, that when Lindsay's turn comes to vacate the manager's post, it will be done in a different manner. As a member of the board of directors, he should at least be able to see the axe coming.'

At one fell swoop the board had unwittingly unleashed a whirlwind. Even though Bob Ashby was angry at the turn of events he still failed to carry out a damage limitation strategy by issuing a statement of appeasement. Instead he responded by saying that my reaction was a case of sour grapes and that the best man for the job had been appointed.

In my view the board should and could have pursued a totally different strategy. If they had felt it necessary to make changes, then adopting a patronising, 'we know best' approach was guaranteed to invite criticism. In drawing up new criteria for the job the board should first have taken me into their confidence, thanked me for past services and made a public statement announcing its new strategy, inviting applications for the new post. I could then have decided whether or not to apply for the new post, and Maurice Lindsay would not have been placed in the untenable position of first being privy to the discussions and then finding himself elected to the position of manager. In the event it came across as a change that had been rushed through with undue haste. The board decided to bring control of international rugby within its remit, and I was an anomaly because I had been appointed before the board had been formed. I enjoyed too much autonomy, if you like.

I needed to do one more thing before I could get on with the rest of my life, and that was to express my views at the Rugby Football League council. I prefaced my remarks by saying that they were not directed personally at Maurice Lindsay, and I wished him well. I did, however, review my period of office and criticised the board for the manner in which it had conducted the affair. A vote of thanks was proposed and minuted, and I felt a sense of relief that I had been able to express myself frankly within the council chamber. I think that perhaps the board were also relieved that it had been finally raised and considered in a proper manner. I did not harbour any bitterness or resentment against them; I was able to look each of them in the eye and hoped that they could do the same to me.

Perhaps it is for someone else to put my period of office into perspective, but I believe that there were several notable achievements. First and foremost were the crucial appointments of two dedicated, if contrasting coaches in Maurice Bamford and Mal Reilly. They were equally committed to the cause of international rugby and approached the task with confidence and enthusiasm. They were supported by Phil Larder whose contribution was wide-ranging. His statistical analysis of matches and players provided important data, but his views on team preparation and tactics were also respected by both coaches. Between us we laid down a long-term strategy for overall player development, investing in immediate and future needs. Fitness testing and monitoring programmes were introduced with advice to players on training schedules, diet and mental preparation. By involving players in the process, by inviting them to express views and discuss tactics we attempted to raise their levels of understanding and awareness.

Back in 1985 Great Britain based its overall game plan on four key areas: defence, support, control and kicking. These were fundamental to the Australian game and we adapted them to our use. Now every club in Great Britain works on these key areas in team preparation.

Coaching standards at international level in my time were excellent, with every session planned in fine detail. Team meetings, video analysis and motivational films became the norm, and international players came to expect and demand first-class preparations which also included physiotherapy and medical treatment, accommodation and kit. No detail was left to chance. Part of our plan was based on continuity, with the establishment of an élite squad of quality players in an effort to minimise team changes. This gave stability to the national side with the emphasis on developing a 'club' atmosphere.

Alongside the progressive raising of playing standards came increased media support and interest, and they in turn projected a positive image to the public about what we were attempting to achieve. The game became more marketable as its image improved, which in turn attracted increased sponsorship.

We still have some way to go but the investment is beginning to pay off. I am proud to have been associated with the whole enterprise. I know how much effort has been put in since 1985 to reverse the downward trend, and the epic win in Sydney in 1988 and victory over the 1989 Kiwis were clear proof of progress. Historians will, I believe, look back on the 1980s and mark it as a watershed in our game, when our fortunes at international level took a definite upswing.

Andy Platt established himself as one of Great Britain's most powerful forwards on the Lions tour of 1988. Moving up to prop in the 1989 series against New Zealand, he continued to show an astonishing work rate.

8

Under New Management

Maurice Lindsay's appointment heralded the start of a crucial and demand-ing year for Great Britain's international team, with no less than ten Test matches to be completed against France, Papua New Guinea, New Zealand, and the ultimate challenge, Australia. The outcome of these engagements would determine whether or not the renaissance of British Rugby League was fact or fiction after a five-year period of active reform and restructuring at all levels throughout the game. Optimism was high following the successful British Coal Test series against the Kiwis in the autumn of 1989, although the timing of the tour to Papua New Guinea and New Zealand prior to the visit of the Kangaroos was far from ideal.

My period of influence as manager was now over, and coming to terms with that fact was not easy. No one is indispensable, however, and sooner or later all of those in positions of influence or authority within the game have to relinquish the reins. Now I would have to sit back and view the international scene like any other Rugby League enthusiast. My desire for Great Britain's success was in no way diminished, but I knew that the withdrawal symptoms would eventually subside just as they had when I retired from playing and stepped down from club coaching. The process is no less painful, whatever the circumstances.

Before the 1990 Lions tour was to start, Maurice Lindsay had an ideal opportunity to prepare himself for his additional responsibilities with the two traditional Tests against France. His approach would be different, but he was inheriting two vastly experienced international coaches in Mal Reilly and Phil Larder, and a strong squad of players. As a matter of fact Maurice, on behalf of Wigan, had legitimately plundered the international squad during my period as manager in his quest for club supremacy. His shopping list had included Ellery Hanley, Andy Goodway, Andy Gregory, Joe Lydon, Andy Platt and Kelvin Skerrett – the cream of British Rugby League. Add to those Kevin Iro, Dean Bell and Adrian Shelford from New Zealand, and a few sparkling gems from Australia such as Brett Kenny and John Ferguson, and the key to Wigan's success is not too difficult to discover. The signing of outstanding junior talent such as Shaun Edwards, Denis Betts, Bobby Goulding, Phil Clarke, Ian Lucas and Ian Gildart are gilt-edged securities for the future. As a full-time administrator with the world's top club Maurice was to make the transition to Great Britain manager without disrupting the system of selection, preparation and coaching that was already in place. In time he would, of course, introduce his own ideas and refinements but his first objective was to get to know the coaches and to observe. As a member of the board of directors he would certainly have greater access to financial resources should he need them.

France, under more stable management at governing-body level, were beginning to respond to their extrovert coach, Jacques Jorda. There had been a few false dawns before, but the word coming from informed opinion was that France had assembled a pretty useful squad and had invested heavily in their preparation. Great Britain, however, were hardly in a period of decline, so victories over France were confidently predicted.

The first British Coal Test match was played on 18 March in Perpignan, where France had enjoyed success against Great Britain in the past, losing only one of their six previous internationals there. In 1985 France had gained ample revenge after a 50–4 thrashing by Maurice Bamford's team at Headingley when I was first appointed manager. The return match was in Perpignan, and the French cut us down to size with a 24–16 victory. The Great Britain management were more than aware of the unpredictability of the French and the danger of complacency, and selected the strongest available side.

Wigan youngster Denis Betts was denied an early Test début against the 1989 Kiwis by injury, but came through to win his first cap against France in 1990 and lay claim to a permanent berth in the Test team's second row.

In the event, Great Britain were distinctly fortunate to come away with an 8–4 victory. It looked deceptively easy in the early stages as Martin Offiah strolled in unopposed from forty metres out, but injuries to Loughlin and Platt followed shortly afterwards and, well though their débutant replacements, Daryl Powell and Denis Betts, performed, the disruption gave heart to the French. With Divet and Cabestany a constant threat, and half-backs Dumas and Entat controlling the play, they deserved their place in the running when Dumas ran around Entat on Great Britain's 22 and lobbed a huge pass out to Pons, who scored in the corner. It was only France's woeful goal-kicking and the intervention of referee Stokes, who disallowed tries by Delaunay, following Fraisse's devastating break, and Dumas, that prevented them claiming the match. With the fit-again Hanley subdued and only Skerrett enhancing his reputation, Great Britain were dependent on Schofield's two penalty goals to clinch their victory.

France: Pougeau; Ratier, Fraisse, Delaunay, Pons; Dumas, Entat; Rabot, Valéro, Buttignol, Divet, Cabestany, Moliner
   Substitutes: Aillères for Buttignol after 70 minutes; Ruiz, Bienes and Sokolow not used
   Scorer: try – Pons

Great Britain: Tait (Widnes); Lydon (Wigan), Schofield (Leeds), Loughlin (St Helens), Offiah (Widnes); Edwards (Wigan), Andy Gregory (Wigan); Skerrett (Bradford Northern), Kevin Beardmore (Castleford), Platt (Wigan), Mike Gregory (Warrington), Goodway (Wigan), Hanley (Wigan)
   Substitutes: Daryl Powell (Sheffield Eagles) for Loughlin after 5 minutes, Betts (Wigan) for Platt after 23 minutes; Steadman (Castleford) and England (Castleford) not used
   Scorers: try – Offiah; goals – Schofield (2)

Referee: J. Stokes (New Zealand)

A post-match discussion with Mal Reilly confirmed my opinion that two factors had counted against us. First and foremost the French attitude, commitment and enthusiasm had been superior because they were desperate for success whereas our players were not particularly excited at the prospect of beating France – it was just another match. Although the coaches had done everything to counter this negative and complacent attitude the players were coming to the end of a long, hard season and many of them had been involved in emotional and energy-sapping cup-ties the previous weekend. Put these two factors together, and you have the potential for disaster.

The return match was at Headingley on 7 April and Great Britain were forced to make several changes because of injury to key players. Out went Andy Gregory, Hanley, Platt, Goodway, Loughlin and Lydon. In came

Carl Gibson, Graham Steadman, Keith England, Karl Fairbank and the former Cardiff Rugby Union winger, Gerald Cordle, in his first season with Bradford Northern. Maurice Lindsay announced, 'This time we know what to expect and, although we have been decimated by injuries, we have still got a quality side and we are looking for a big performance.'

After twenty minutes' play, everything was going according to plan. The French had made enough errors under pressure to allow Great Britain two tries, first Schofield putting Cordle on an unstoppable run to the corner and then Betts unloading in the tackle to Tait, who stormed through a gap to score. Yet again the prompting of Dumas and Entat brought France back as their error count dropped and their tackles became more determined. Pons exploited Cordle's defensive uncertainty for a try, and goals by Dumas and Fraisse pulled the score back to 12–8 at half-time. In the second half Rabot and the impressive Divet added further tries, and the control exerted by loose forward Moliner and hooker Valéro meant that France completely dominated Great Britain in all departments. Edwards, captain for the first time, and Steadman paled by comparison with their opposite numbers; Gibson and Schofield sank into anonymity; and the pack were simply outclassed. Offiah's late try brought no significant compensation, and the ecstasy with which the French reacted to their 25–18 victory was well received by the generous crowd.

Great Britain: Tait (Widnes); Cordle (Bradford Northern), Schofield (Leeds), Gibson (Leeds), Offiah (Widnes); Steadman (Castleford), Edwards (Wigan); Skerrett (Bradford Northern), Kevin Beardmore (Castleford), England (Castleford), Betts (Wigan), Fairbank (Bradford Northern), Mike Gregory (Warrington)
Substitutes: Irwin (Castleford) for Cordle after 55 minutes, Bishop (Hull KR) for Skerrett after 61 minutes; Fox (Featherstone Rovers) and Roy Powell (Leeds) not used
Scorers: tries – Cordle, Tait, Offiah; goals – Steadman (3)

France: Fraisse; Ratier, Delaunay, Bienes, Pons; Dumas, Entat; Buttignol, Valéro, Rabot, Divet, Cabestany, Moliner
Substitutes: Frison for Cabestany after 77 minutes; Sokolow, Tisseyre and Marquet not used
Scorers: tries – Pons, Rabot, Divet; goals – Fraisse (5), Dumas; drop-goal – Dumas

Referee: J. Stokes (New Zealand)

If I had missed being in the Great Britain dressing-room before the match I was relieved that I was not required to be there afterwards. I knew that the gloom and depression would be oppressive, and that Maurice Lindsay and Mal Reilly would be attempting to explain the defeat to the press, who in turn were not sure whether to be excited by the French revival or critical of Britain's failure. If enthusiasm and commitment had been lacking in Perpignon they had been totally absent at Headingley – just as Mal Reilly and Phil Larder were looking for a confidence-boosting display before selecting the tour squad. For one or two players the display was to cost them dear and to mark the end of their international careers.

The task of assembling a squad for the 1990 tour must have led to many moments of depression and frustration for the Great Britain management as top-class players fell like leaves in autumn. Personal reasons, family reasons, injury and imminent surgery were all legitimate excuses, and yet Maurice Lindsay and Mal Reilly must have believed that they were rearranging deck chairs on the *Titanic*. The list of players unavailable for selection included Hanley, Andy Gregory, Edwards, Platt, Hampson, Les Holliday, Des Drummond, and Lydon and Offiah, who both eventually joined the party in New Zealand. Despite these set-backs, however, a squad was assembled which, in the main, received approval because of its emphasis on youth; the average age of the squad was 23. Nevertheless there was also criticism that some of the squad had but limited professional experience, some showed only fitful form for their clubs, and some relied strongly on reputations established during their days in Rugby Union.

The final squad was:

Denis Betts (Wigan)	Shaun Irwin (Castleford)
Chris Bibb (Featherstone Rovers)	Lee Jackson (Hull)
David Bishop (Hull KR)	Ian Lucas (Wigan)
Phil Clarke (Wigan)	Daryl Powell (Sheffield Eagles)
Jonathan Davies (Widnes)	Roy Powell (Leeds)
Martin Dermott (Wigan)	Gary Price (Wakefield Trinity)
Paul Dixon (Leeds)	Garry Schofield (Leeds)
Paul Eastwood (Hull)	Roger Simpson (Bradford Northern)
Keith England (Castleford)	Kelvin Skerrett (Bradford Northern)
Karl Fairbank (Bradford Northern)	Ian Smales (Featherstone Rovers)
Deryck Fox (Featherstone Rovers)	Graham Steadman (Castleford)
Carl Gibson (Leeds)	Tony Sullivan (Hull KR)
Bobby Goulding (Wigan)	Alan Tait (Widnes)
Mike Gregory (Warrington)	

Mal Reilly announced, 'On this summer's tour, we've chosen to go for a youth policy. The young players can develop on tour and potentially have a lot more scope than the older, more experienced players. We're still going out there to win, but along the way we also have a chance to develop young players who will stand Great Britain in good stead in the next four or five years.'

Shorn of his top players Mal would use the time at his disposal before the Kiwi Tests to good effect. He would need that time to identify his best combination and to raise levels of fitness and tactical awareness. He still had a strong nucleus of experienced internationals (Schofield, Fairbank, Mike Gregory, Roy Powell), and these would form the core of his team. Mike Gregory was appointed tour captain, a role he fulfilled with distinction. Although he was third choice Mike did not allow that to deter him as he said with bursting pride, 'I've achieved my ambition of playing at Wembley, I've played everywhere in the world and now I'm going to captain a touring team; I'm honoured.'

Castleford's world-record signing from Featherstone Rovers, Graham Steadman, made an inauspicious Test bow against France at Leeds in 1990. He still won selection for the summer tour, but injury in New Zealand reduced his chances of making an impact.

The 1990 Lions departed on Monday 13 May determined to prove the critics wrong. Despite gloomy predictions of impending doom the whole party had a defiant mood and a steely determination to succeed. Early tour reports confirmed that there was an excellent spirit within the Great Britain camp, and that the management was working hard to keep the players occupied. Certainly events in Papua New Guinea had changed dramatically since 1988 and the capital, Port Moresby, was now experiencing an unprecedented wave of crime and violence. This meant a

curfew for the players, as to go about at night was to invite mugging. The
players responded by establishing a social committee to devise a programme
of activities to offset boredom. The special camaraderie that tour parties
develop is essential for success, and the 1990 Lions were no exception.
This bond was to sustain them throughout the whole tour and was to prove
indestructible.

Great Britain kicked off the tour confidently with a 40–18 victory over
Southern Zone. In 1984 Ronnie Duane was injured in the first match
of the Lions tour and took no further part. In 1988 Shaun Edwards
lasted fifteen minutes. The 1990 Lions were no different, except that
young Anthony Sullivan was injured in training and had to return home
without playing a game. When it was discovered that Skerrett needed
surgery in Australia on an injured knee, John Devereux, the former Wales
Rugby Union international from Widnes, was summoned to join the tour
as replacement.

The second match against Northern Highlands was tougher, and the
tourists were not entirely happy with a 24–10 victory. Nevertheless, two wins
had put the Lions in good heart, and the coaches had had an opportunity
to assess the squad and decide on the best combination. There had been
encouraging signs from two of the controversial selections, ex-Rugby Union
star Jonathan Davies and teenage half-back Bobby Goulding while Dixon,
lively hooker Lee Jackson and Mike Gregory had showed great appetites
for work, despite the intense heat.

Interest in the first British Coal Test at Garoka in the Highlands was at
fever pitch. Great Britain, however, were more apprehensive about playing at
5,000 feet, as altitude was an unknown factor. On the day of the match, extra
police were called in as thousands of fans congregated outside the Danny
Leaky stadium, unable to gain admission. The Great Britain team had to
force their way through a colourful and turbulent crowd, many of whom
were wearing tribal costume and carrying fearsome-looking weapons. None
of this was designed to calm the players nerves and is hardly recommended
pre-match preparation.

Paul Eastwood gave Great Britain an early lead with a try from Tait's
pass, but after only fourteen minutes stone-throwing supporters, denied
access to the ground, stormed the fences in an effort to break in. The
police retaliated with tear-gas, and the referee and players stood bemused
as swirling, stinging clouds enveloped them in the centre of the pitch.

Within seconds of the restart following these horror-movie scenes,
Great Britain conceded a try to the Papuan prop, Evei. Veteran centre
Numapo piled on the pressure with a penalty goal and, as the Kumuls
pounded the British line, Horu slipped over for a second try. Davies
and Goulding responded with splendid opportunist tries, but a string of
penalties awarded by the harassed referee, Dennis Hale, largely on the
advice of two less-than-impartial touch-judges, kept Papua ahead of the
game. At the end of the day, despite the sterling efforts of Jackson, it was

the inability of Schofield and Goulding to dictate the play and the lack of commitment shown by too many players that were responsible for the Lions' 18–20 defeat.

Papua New Guinea: Wanega; Krewanty, Boge, Numapo, Morea; Horu, Ongugo; Ako, Matmillo, Evei, Gupe, Taumaku, Angra
Substitutes: Arigae for Ako after 45 minutes, Kool for Goge after 52 minutes; Iram and Jin not used
Scorer: tries – Evei, Horu; goals – Numapo (5); drop-goals – Numapo, Horu

Great Britain: Tait (Widnes); Eastwood (Hull), Daryl Powell (Sheffield Eagles), Davies (Widnes), Gibson (Leeds); Schofield (Leeds), Goulding (Wigan); Roy Powell (Leeds), Jackson (Hull), Dixon (Leeds), Betts (Wigan), Fairbank (Bradford Northern), Mike Gregory (Warrington)
Substitutes: Irwin (Castleford) for Daryl Powell after 38 minutes, England (Castleford) for Fairbank after 50 minutes; Fox (Featherstone Rovers) and Clarke (Wigan) not used
Scorers: tries – Eastwood, Davies, Goulding; goals – Davies (3)

Referee: D. Hale (New Zealand)

A 50–4 victory over the Islands Zone, with two tries from Devereux and strong showings from Fox, Clarke and England, put heart back into the Lions, but even that match was disrupted by panicking spectators invading the pitch in an effort to escape the inevitable tear-gas. The players must have thought they were front-line troops in a war zone, and had a right to expect campaign medals on their return to England. In future people would be able to point them out and say, 'He was on the Tear-Gas Tour.' Certainly future tourists will have to be protected from such events if Papua New Guinea is to continue to host tours. The country is beautiful and exotic, the people friendly and hospitable, but if the highly volatile nature of the crowds is to put players at risk then we have a duty to protect them.

Tension and nerves built up in the British camp in preparation for the second British Coal Test, particularly when late fitness tests were required on England and Daryl Powell. But Mal demonstrated confidence in the team when he made only one change from the first Test by replacing Fairbank with England. This time they knew what to expect and prepared for every eventuality – including tear-gas.

The atmosphere of the second Test was different in every way from that of the first, from the more civilised surroundings of Port Moresby to the grim determination of the Lions to have their revenge. The forwards led by example, with Dixon, England and Roy Powell tackling ferociously and making huge inroads around the ruck, while Betts and Gregory offered pace and penetration further out. It was an easy task for the backs to feed off this platform, Eastwood finishing off a slick move by Davies and Daryl Powell as early as the sixth minute and Gibson finishing strongly on the opposite flank to crown skilful approach work first by Gregory, Schofield and Tait, and then by the speedy Davies. There were further tries for both half-backs, the unsung Daryl Powell and the deserving Dixon. Although the Lions complained afterwards about the effect of the blazing heat, it seemed that the Kumuls suffered more; the final result, a 40–8 victory for Great Britain, suggests that the Papuan players had celebrated their first Test win not wisely, but too well.

Papua New Guinea: Wanega; Krewanty, Boge, Numapo, Morea; Horu, Ongugo; Lomutopa, Matmillo, Evei, Gupe, Taumaku, Angra
Substitutes: Tiri for Lomutopa after 45 minutes, Iram for Morea after 55 minutes; Kool and Arigae not used
Scorers: try – Ongugo; goals – Numapo (2)

Great Britain: Tait (Widnes); Eastwood (Hull), Davies (Widnes), Daryl Powell (Sheffield Eagles), Gibson (Leeds); Schofield (Leeds), Goulding (Wigan); Roy Powell (Leeds), Jackson (Hull), England (Catleford), Dixon (Leeds), Betts (Wigan), Mike Gregory (Warrington)

Substitutes: Fox (Featherstone Rovers) for Jackson after 37 minutes, Clarke (Wigan) for Mike Gregory after 57 minutes; Irwin (Castleford) and Fairbank (Bradford Northern) not used

Scorers: tries – Gibson (2), Goulding, Dixon, Daryl Powell, Schofield, Eastwood; goals – Davies (6)

Referee: D. Hale (New Zealand)

The Lions cheered as they flew out of Port Moresby for a relaxing break in Cairns in Northern Queensland. The contrast to Papua New Guinea came as a welcome relief for everyone in the party, and they threw themselves enthusiastically into trips to the Great Barrier Reef and raft excursions down raging rivers. 'Threw' is the operative word, as in true Rambo fashion Mal Reilly elected to travel down the most dangerous stretch of river outside the dinghy; not exactly recommended! The short break was also used to put finishing touches to the players' general conditioning before the New Zealand leg, and the team were reunited with Kelvin Skerrett following a successful operation on his troublesome knee.

Although touring New Zealand is not prized as highly as touring Australia the party was actually breaking new ground as previous tours there had always followed a strenuous programme of matches in Australia. They would certainly need a positive frame of mind if they were to win the Test series in New Zealand, as Great Britain had not done this for eleven years. Although the Lions were not at full strength, there was every reason to be optimistic because New Zealand had not got the overall quality of player that had been available between 1980 and 1987, and were still in the process of deciding on their best combination. They were at home, however, and traditional Kiwi pride made them formidable opponents.

The opening match of the New Zealand leg of the tour ended with a 23–22 victory over a very strong President's XIII. The hero of the day was hooker Martin Dermott who snatched a last-minute victory with a drop-goal, but it was the Kiwi back-rowers, Kuiti and Leota, and the powerful winger, Sam Panapa, who gave notice of their imminent threat to the Lions' hopes. A disappointing crowd figure of 5,000 did not augur well for the Great Britain coffers, and as the tour progressed there was increasing concern expressed by Maurice Lindsay at the sparse attendances, poor marketing and low-key staging of matches by the New Zealand board, in some instances at totally inappropriate venues. Future Great Britain tours would be looking for financial guarantees which in turn would promote a more concerted effort by the hosts to increase revenue.

Despite all the work of the coaches to remedy the problem, the Lions demonstrated alarming traits of inconsistency, just as they had done in 1988. A 10–18 defeat in Canterbury increased the pressure on Mal Reilly who was desperate to string together a morale-boosting set of wins before taking on the Kiwis. Only a brilliant solo effort by Rugby Union convert David Bishop

Opposite Castleford's Keith England proved to be a gritty, dependable performer on the Lions' summer tour in 1990, and stiffened up the pack considerably when slotted in at blind-side prop after the unexpected defeat by Papua New Guinea.

and a lucky try from Alan Tait near the end gave the score an element of respectability.

A further defeat against Auckland by 10–24 added to the management's woes, particularly as Great Britain fielded their likely Test team. In a scrappy, niggling match scarred by skirmishes between half-backs Goulding and Stu Galbraith, the efforts of Gregory, England and Gibson kept the Lions in the lead for an hour before Panapa reappeared to haunt them with a try that took Auckland clear in the final quarter. The Kiwi press were already sensing victory in the British Coal Tests, and Graham Lowe was reported in the *Sydney Daily Telegraph* as saying, 'The New Zealanders will win the series 3–0, and that is not an old Kiwi coach talking from the heart. The Great Britain side was in a tattered state when it left for the tour because of the huge number of stars who were not available. Injuries on tour have further reduced the potency of a young side of good players lacking international experience. The Kiwis are red-hot favourites to whitewash the Poms.'

Despite those set-backs, however, the British camp continued to issue positive statements of intent as they schemed and plotted to produce a shock. A 22–10 victory over the Kiwi Colts three days before the first Test was a welcome boost, and there was some speculation that Davies, who outplayed Kelly Shelford, the Kiwis' 1989 Test stand-off, might be selected as a half-back partner for Goulding. Mal refused to be panicked, however, and he stuck with players of proven international experience when he named his Test side. Because of a persistent groin strain, Alan Tait had been flown home, and so Chris Bibb claimed the full-back position while David Lyon of Warington was summoned as a replacement. Davies was exiled on the wing to accomodate the newly-arrived Joe Lydon, and Gibson moved infield to vacate Offiah's left-wing berth. Skerrett was to play at prop, and Martin Demott won a deserved first cap as hooker.

The team was a mixture of Under-21 and full internationals, of youth and experience. The question was, was it good enough to win? My experience told me that the coaches would go for a simple game plan based on an eager defence, particularly around the play-the-ball. The pack was not over-blessed with skilful ball-players, but each member was fit and committed, and I knew that Mal and Phil would not encourage them to play flashy football or take unnecessary risks until a solid platform had been achieved. Joe Lydon and Garry Schofield in particular would have responsibility for pumping the ball down the field to gain territory which would have to be secured by a good chase. Attitude, commitment, discipline and courage would be at the heart of the strategy; without these to underpin tactics, victory at Test match level cannot be achieved.

After twenty minutes of the first British Coal Test, the writing was on the wall for Mal's new-look Great Britain team. In only the second minute that man Sam Panapa had crashed through Chris Bibb's despairing tackle for the opening try following good work by McGahan and Nikau.

Although Schofield made a searing midfield break to lay on a superb try for Davies and keep the Lions in contention, Kevin Iro's disputed try and Peter Brown's conversion threatened to open the floodgates of an ominously vulnerable defence. Yet time and again it was the invaluable Paul Dixon, backed up by Gregory, Dermott and even Schofield, who pulled off a crucial tackle to plug the gap and deny the Kiwis. Having worked wonders to keep his side in the match, Dixon then popped up on the end of a blistering fifty-metre break by the outstanding Schofield five minutes into the second half, to give the scoring pass to their Leeds club-mate Gibson. Schofield then tagged on a drop-goal to give Great Britain a slender, 1-point advantage and, as the Lions came more and more into the match, Offiah burst away with an interception, only to be called back for some mysterious infringement. The match ended with the Kiwis a spent force, having squandered all their first-half superiority, and the Lions in the ascendant, in celebration of their 11–10 victory.

New Zealand: Williams; Tony Iro, Kevin Iro, Kemp, Panapa; Clark, Freeman; Brown, Duane Mann, Todd, Nikau, Mark Horo, McGahan
Substitutes: George Mann for Todd after 60 minutes, Edwards for Tony Iro after 69 minutes; Nixon and Lonergan not used
Scorers: tries – Panapa, Kevin Iro; goal – Brown

Great Britain: Bibb (Featherstone Rovers); Davies (Widnes), Lydon (Wigan), Gibson (Leeds), Offiah (Widnes); Schofield (Leeds), Goulding (Wigan); Skerrett (Bradford Northern), Dermott (Wigan), England (Castleford), Dixon (Leeds), Betts (Wigan), Mike Gregory (Warrington)
Substitutes: Roy Powell (Leeds) for Skerrett after 55 minutes, Daryl Powell (Sheffield Eagles) for Lydon after 62 minutes; Fox (Featherstone Rovers) and Lucas (Wigan) not used
Scorers: tries – Davies; Gibson; goal – Davies; drop-goal – Schofield

Referee: D. Manson (Australia)

The delight on the faces of the British players as they hugged each other must have been a pleasure to see as, once again, against all the odds they had come through to gain a superb Test victory. When I rang Mal to congratulate him a few hours later it was as a friend, but he shared his feelings with me and I could sense the immense relief and elation he was experiencing. My personal feeling was that Great Britain could only get better, whereas the Kiwis could just have shot their bolt.

The mood was shortlived, however, as the Lions stumbled to a 22–30 defeat against Wellington the following Wednesday in front of only 800 spectators on a rain-drenched afternoon. Despite a 22–8 half-time lead, with tries by Fairbank and Ian Smales and a brilliant forty-five-metre effort

by Davies, Great Britain went into steep decline after the interval in the face of a stern challenge from Howie Tamati's men, led effectively by Kiwi reject Mike Kuiti. The defeat suggested that, as in Australia in 1988, many of those outside the Test team were some way short of the required standard.

Before the second British Coal Test Great Britain had to take on the New Zealand Maoris, who had been preparing for battle by following the ancient tribal practice of sleeping in a communal hut. It was expected to be a tough encounter but skipper Mike Gregory inspired a near-Test team to an impressive 20–12 victory, crowning his efforts with a long break from inside his own 22 before passing to Paul Eastwood to score a sensational try. For Mike it must have conjured up memories of his epic try against Australia in the famous third Test victory in Sydney. He had been troubled with a damaged ankle throughout the tour, but always managed to train and play without complaint.

By now it was clear that the New Zealand leg of the tour was to be a financial disaster. Maurice Lindsay had projected an £80,000 overall budget deficit; this was now looking like a conservative estimate. There is no way that Rugby League in New Zealand could ever displace Rugby Union in terms of support, finance or media interest, but it maintains a reasonably high profile because of television. Top-class matches are screened weekly from the Sydney competition – arguably the highest quality rugby of either code in the world. Few people actually watch Rugby League at club level in New Zealand, but the system produces a great many talented players who must migrate to Australia and Great Britain for fame and fortune. The television exposure poses a dilemma, and Ray French, the BBC commentator, is worried about over-exposure and its long-term effect on the development of Rugby League in New Zealand. He points to the fact that less than 16,000 spectators attended the three Test matches, and yet the first Test was only marginally behind the All Blacks v. Scotland Rugby Union international in the TV ratings. Until Rugby League's popularity in the country can be reckoned in terms of gate receipts from paying customers, there will always be questions surrounding the future of the game in New Zealand.

The Kiwis threw themselves into their preparations for the second Test with total commitment, believing that complacency had led to their downfall. Hugh McGahan, the captain, foolishly fuelled the Lions' preparation by criticising their style of play as boring. It was a remark that merely demonstrated that the Kiwis' confidence and self-belief had been badly dented. Mal Reilly knew he had a depleted hand of players, but nevertheless he and Phil Larder had devised a defensive game plan which had brought victory. It was up to Bob Bailey, the Kiwi coach, to find a way of breaking down that Lions defence.

An incident which involved Great Britain scrum-half Bobby Goulding grabbed the headlines and threatened to disrupt the Lions' preparation.

Opposite Martin Offiah and Kiwi full-back Darrell Williams are locked in a strange dance in search of a descending ball. Williams lost his place for the second and third Tests in 1990 to Rugby Union convert Matthew Ridge, whose goal-kicking nearly saved the series for New Zealand.

Goulding was charged with assaulting two New Zealanders in an Auckland restaurant and was subsequently given a conditional discharge by the district court; he was also subject to some internal disciplinary action by the Great Britain management, although no sanctions were reported by the press. Several months later Goulding appeared before the board of directors, charged with bringing the game into disrepute. Although found guilty of the charge a severe reprimand was thought to be an appropriate punishment.

This contrasted starkly with the severe punishment meted out to Joe Lydon and Des Drummond when they were withdrawn from the 1988 Lions tour by the Rugby Football League for disciplinary reasons. This was favourably commented on at the time by the British press as being essential if the good name of Rugby League was to be protected. The same press, however, responded to this incident with a deafening silence. Goulding not only escaped censure and suspension, but actually represented Great Britain a few days after his court appearance.

Bobby is a player with a precocious talent who has burst onto the rugby scene like a small meteor, and was exclusively responsible for the anonymity of Gary Freeman in the first Test. To play in all five Tests on the tour was a remarkable achievement, and a glittering career lies ahead. I'm sure he now recognises his good fortune and, as a result, will be better equipped to handle the pressures of being a top sportsman – and those pressures will increase in future years both on and off the field.

The governing body, however, has a duty to protect the image of the game, and in recent years the board of directors have been both vigilant and active in clamping down on players and officials found guilty of bringing the game into disrepute. They have been particularly active in promoting Rugby League as a family game, backed up by a strict disciplinary committee who have dished out eight-match suspensions for violent behaviour on the field of play. Yet consistency has to be at the heart of any disciplinary process if it is to maintain credibility. Double standards cannot be sanctioned, otherwise dangerous precedents will undermine the whole structure. Rugby League is the envy of many other sports for the decisive way it keeps its house in order, but, to quote Winston Churchill, 'the price of freedom is eternal vigilance.'

None of this was allowed to disrupt the Lions' preparation, as they remained single-minded in their determination to win the British Coal Test series. As Mal Reilly put the finishing touches to his Test team, Phil Larder took the second string to New Plymouth for a match against a Taranaki XIII, which was won in some style by 24–0. Fox, Bishop and Eastwood showed outstanding form, and there were tries for Roger Simpson, David Lyon, Karl Fairbank and Shaun Irwin.

The Kiwis stuck to the same line-up for the second Test, except for the full-back position where they took a calculated gamble in selecting the former All Black, Matthew Ridge, who had only recently turned professional with Manly. Great Britain also changed full-backs with the more experi-

Bradford Northern prop Kelvin Skerrett was one of the great successes for Great Britain in the 1989-90 season, and his recovery from injury on the 1990 summer tour was a vital factor in the Lions' victory over New Zealand.

enced Joe Lydon replacing Chris Bibb. Daryl Powell returned in Lydon's place in the centre, and Jackson replaced the injured Dermott at hooker.

It was another match where New Zealand's superiority often appeared to be overwhelming, but a combination of their own profligacy and Great Britain's magnificent defence conspired to rob them of victory. Always the final pass went astray, or the wrong option was taken, or Dixon or Schofield or Gregory would produce a rat-trap tackle to quash a half-chance. All the while there lurked the threat of Schofield, poised to strike with decisive force and claim the match for the Lions. So it happened after half an hour, when the stand-off sold an exquisite dummy twenty metres from the New Zealand line to race home and cancel out Ridge's early penalties. After fifty-five minutes, Schofield broke again, this time out of Brown's impotent tackle, to send in Betts, once more to outstrip Ridge's goal-kicking for a 12–8 lead. But Mark Horo levelled the scores on the end of a Nikau break, and Ridge's fifth goal gave the Kiwis an advantage which they looked like retaining until the end. Yet with only seven minutes left on the clock, Kelvin Skerrett led a final surge upfield before slipping the ball out of the tackle on his own 22 to the keenly supporting Daryl Powell. Powell was away on a thirty-metre spurt, drawing the full-back before timing his pass out to Offiah with perfection. It's been said that, in a foot-race, you always come second to Martin Offiah, and so, for all the valiant efforts of the covering Kevin Iro, there was no stopping the Widnes flier as he sped to the corner to win the match by 16–14 and the British Coal series by 2–0.

New Zealand: Ridge; Panapa, Kevin Iro, Williams, Tony Iro; Clark, Freeman; Brown, Duane Mann, Todd, Nikau, Mark Horo, McGahan
    Substitutes: Lonergan for Todd and Kemp for Clark after 76 minutes; Edwards and George Mann not used
    Scorers: try – Mark Horo; goals – Ridge (5)

Great Britain: Lydon (Wigan); Davies (Widnes), Gibson (Leeds), Daryl Powell (Sheffield Eagles), Offiah (Widnes); Schofield (Leeds), Goulding (Wigan); Skerrett (Bradford Northern), Jackson (Hull), England (Castleford), Dixon (Leeds), Betts (Wigan), Mike Gregory (Warrington)
    Substitutes: Irwin (Castleford) for Gibson after 59 minutes, Roy Powell (Leeds) for Dixon after 67 minutes; Fox (Featherstone Rovers) and Fairbank (Bradford Northern) not used
    Scorers: tries – Schofield, Betts, Offiah; goals – Davies (2)

Referee: W. Harrigan (Australia)

The Lions were jubilant and totally convinced that they could whitewash New Zealand 3–0. In any case, victory in the third British Coal Test was vital because it was a World Cup qualifying match. The Kiwis brought in Tony Kemp at stand-off, while for Great Britain Paul Dixon could feel some injustice at being replaced by Roy Powell, and Lee Jackson fell victim to Mal's preference for Martin Dermott's organisational ability around the ruck.

Martin Offiah, the hero of the second Test, took just three minutes to undo all that good work and, in the event, cost Great Britain the third Test. Good work by Gregory and Daryl Powell had sent Goulding haring through a gap, and he put Offiah clear to the posts. But the winger, seeking a nonchalant, one-handed touchdown, saw the ball slip from his grasp and referee Harrigan rule a knock-on; the chance was gone. When Schofield dummied his way over and Davies added a penalty, the error did not appear all that crucial, but steadily the Lions' concentration waned and the Kiwis stormed back with tries from Kemp and Nikau and five goals from the unerring boot of Ridge. A deficit of 6–18 at half-time was a mountain for Great Britain to climb.

The Lions' fight-back was conducted in a heated second half, with Goulding, Schofield and McGahan all finding their way to the sin bin. Before his departure, Schofield sent the tireless Roy Powell in for a try, and when Offiah atoned in part for his earlier blunder by squeezing round Tony Iro and Ridge into the corner, it looked as though Great Britain might just snatch victory. But McGahan's drop-goal widened the margin again by just enough, and the Lions, brave battlers all, ran out of time, 18–21 in arrears.

New Zealand: Ridge; Panapa, Kevin Iro, Williams, Tony Iro; Kemp, Freeman; Brown, Duane Mann, Todd, Nikau, Mark Horo, McGahan
Substitutes: Edwards for Kevin Iro after 45 minutes, Lonergan for Todd after 56 minutes; Clark and George Mann not used
Scorers: tries – Kemp, Nikau; goals – Ridge (6); drop-goal – McGahan

Great Britain: Lydon (Wigan); Davies (Widnes), Gibson (Leeds), Daryl Powell (Sheffield Eagles), Offiah (Widnes); Schofield (Leeds), Goulding (Wigan); Skerrett (Bradford Northern), Dermott (Wigan), England (Castleford), Betts (Wigan), Roy Powell (Leeds), Mike Gregory (Warrington)
Substitutes: Dixon (Leeds) for Skerrett and Irwin (Castleford) for Gibson after 40 minutes; Fox (Featherstone Rovers) and Fairbank (Bradford Northern) not used
Scorers: tries – Schofield, Roy Powell, Offiah; goals – Davies (3)

Referee: W. Harrigan (Australia)

Instead of gaining victory the Lions had to troop off the field angry and frustrated that they had not taken control of the match when it was there for the taking. Nevertheless a series victory had been achieved, and that was a credit to every member of the 1990 Lions tour who had set off ten weeks earlier determined to prove the sceptics wrong.

The Kangaroos preparing to tour Great Britain would have viewed the

Kiwi series with great interest. It confirmed that Great Britain had strength in depth in its international squad, while other experienced Lions were back in England ready to stake their claims for Test places come the autumn. Privately the Great Britain management would admit that the current team was not strong enough to defeat Australia in a Test series. Nevertheless, with Platt, Hanley, Edwards, Andy Gregory, Tait, Loughlin and the Hulme brothers in contention, and maybe one last salvo from Kevin Ward or even Lee Crooks, they were entitled to feel confident that a team strong enough to challenge Australia could be selected. That was three months away; right now the 1990 Lions were entitled to walk tall and enjoy the rest of the summer before girding up their loins for the ultimate challenge of the green-and-golds.

Maurice Lindsay's tour report was highly critical of the Papua New Guinea and New Zealand administration and demanded a thorough investigation before future visits. Certainly, the heavy financial burden carried by the 1990 Lions tour forces one to question the future of the traditional tour pattern. The tour actually cost £471,600 and was only able to recoup £112,279 from gate receipts. New Zealand receipts were as low as £80,000; although I accept that this is a figure well short of expectations I don't believe that New Zealand were ever capable of generating more than £130,000 even with improved marketing. Without British Coal's generous sponsorship and some TV fees the overall losses would have been totally unacceptable to Great Britain.

The Rugby Football League have always been prepared to subsidise tours to Papua New Guinea and New Zealand, but I doubt whether they will carry this burden much longer. When one considers that the 1990 tour costs exceeded those of the 1988 tour by £180,000, the cost of the 1992 tour of Australia could be astronomical. Future tours will probably be restricted to Test matches, with a few lucrative club games in order to maximise income. The world is shrinking and extended tours are no longer necessary to advance the cause of Rugby League. Fortunately we emerged from the tour with a series win. Consider how ludicrous it would have been if we had been defeated. In effect Great Britain would have spent almost half a million pounds to enable New Zealand to demonstrate their superiority over us.

Opposite Martin Offiah's return from injury on the 1990 summer tour meant that he took the position that Paul Eastwood (left) had held in the Tests against Papua New Guinea. However, it was not long before there was room for both of them in the team to face Australia at Wembley.

9

The Final Conflict

The 1990 Kangaroos arrived to much heralded propaganda that they were the finest, not to say the largest, set of players ever to wear the famous green and gold jerseys. Bobby Fulton, their pugnacious coach, who had been a team-mate of Mal Reilly at Manly in the early 1970s, and was a former Test player, made no secret of the fact that they intended to match the 1982 'Invincibles' and return home undefeated.

There was no doubting their size, but had they the creative talent of the 1982 and 1984 Kangaroos? Certainly, the late withdrawal of the legendary Wally Lewis was a factor that benefitted Great Britain. There was also considerable speculation about the quality of the players that Australia had found to replace Sterling, Kenny, Miles and Jack. Players of that calibre only come along at twenty-year intervals, but with Mal Meninga still on board as captain, and rising young players such as Brad Mackay, Laurie Daley and Ricky Stuart alongside such old heads as Steve Roach and Bob Lindner, there was still plenty of food for thought for the Great Britain management.

The Kangaroos opened their account at St Helens with a comfortable 34–4 victory and went on to dispose of Wakefield Trinity in a bad-tempered match by 36–18. When Wigan collapsed, however, at Central Park to the tune of 6–34 the alarm bells began to sound throughout the game. Coach John Monie's injury-weakened team could only sustain resistance for twenty minutes, whereafter the Australian 'mean machine' just rolled over them like Sherman tanks.

What was worrying for Mal Reilly was that several key players had sustained injuries during August and September and were unlikely to be fit for the first British Coal Test. These included Mike Gregory, the captain of the 1990 Lions, Andy Platt, Paul Loughlin, Alan Tait, and Paul Hulme. Several other players, including Kelvin Skerrett and Shaun Edwards, were not showing any convincing club form. Nevertheless, Mal put his faith in men who had served him well in previous campaigns when he announced his team. The only new cap was the Hull prop, Karl Harrison, and there was a final chance for Kevin Ward to make an impact against his old foes.

Informed opinion agreed that it was a solid team, perhaps short on flair. The press latched on to Jonathan Davies's absence, believing that his imagination and pace allied to his kicking skills were essential. Mal, however, pre-ferred the strength and defensive qualities of Paul Eastwood, Daryl Powell and Carl Gibson which left Davies out in the cold and not even substitute. Although he had played in five Tests during the summer there obviously remained a question mark hanging over him like the sword of Damocles.

Great Britain coach Mal Reilly guides his team through a training session in preparation for the first Kangaroo Test at Wembley in 1990. Reilly's homework had been thoroughly done, as the performance of his players was to demonstrate.

Mal also ignored the clamour to select Phil McKenzie, the Widnes hooker. Although McKenzie was Australian by birth, his five-year residency in England had earned him the right to be selected for Great Britain. His ability is outstanding, but Mal, as a proud and patriotic Englishman, perhaps found it difficult to select an Australian ahead of a British player, although he never expressed this view.

It is interesting to reflect on the pace of change when one considers that, of the Great Britain team that played in the final British Coal Test in New Zealand three months earlier, only Dixon, Daryl and Roy Powell, Schofield, Gibson and Offiah survived. At least it proved that there was strength in depth after all. On the other hand eleven of the team had been on the 1988 Lions tour of Australia, so continuity was certainly a central plank of the selection policy.

Great Britain were given a psychological boost when Leeds put up a spirited performance against Australia, eventually losing by 10–22. This was the first serious resistance by a club side for over a decade, and the form of Schofield, Dixon and Gibson in the match gave great encouragement for the Great Britain selection.

The Rugby Football League's board of directors had decided to play the first British Coal Test at Wembley, believing that the occasion justified bold action. Although there was some considerable doubt about the wisdom of the venture, on Saturday 27 October over 50,000 people travelled to London for the match. With half an hour to kick off there were still some gaps in the stadium, and David Oxley, the chief executive, was prowling about looking more than a little anxious. He above all others knew how important it was for the whole venture to be successful, that if the number of spectators didn't meet the pre-match forecast, if Great Britain didn't perform and if the game was a disappointing spectacle then there would be a heavy price to pay in terms of prestige. The spectre of Boothferry Park still haunted all of us; today was to be the day of reckoning.

When the Great Britain team marched out to the emotive strains of *Land of Hope and Glory* there was a quickening of the pulse as waves of patriotic fervour washed over the crowd. The players had been preparing for the challenge for a week, but the real preparation had been taking place for much longer as British Rugby League underwent major surgery for years in a determined effort to reshape itself. Humiliation was no longer acceptable and the Great Britain management and players shouldered this enormous burden of responsibility. I knew Mal was confident, so much so that when I had wished him luck he said, 'When we win, Les, come over to the dressing-room.'

Great Britain kicked off and immediately secured the territorial advantage they were to hold for the majority of the first half by virtue of an Australian handling error. The Kangaroos were simply incapable of raising the siege. Their clearance kicks were confidently swallowed and returned with interest by the excellent Hampson, and the kicking games of Schofield and Andy Gregory worked like clockwork time and again, to drive play deep into the opposition half. As the forward battle developed, it was Dixon, Jackson and Harrison who were getting the upper hand, but at half-time all that Great Britain had to show for their control was a share of a 2–2 scoreline, Eastwood having missed two relatively straightforward penalties.

Those who thought that, as in the first Test in Australia in 1988, Great Britain had shot their bolt were not then prepared for what came after the interval. Skipper Hanley, having a titanic game at loose forward, suddenly wrenched himself out of a half-cock tackle just inside the Australian half and powered away. Just as it seemed that he would go all the way to the corner he was hauled down five metres short, but Daryl Powell was there to take the quick play-the-ball and hand on to Paul Eastwood, who barrelled his way through a forest of legs for the try. No matter the pace and flair of Davies now; Eastwood's place in history was secure.

Yet suddenly the Kangaroos burst into life and an irrepressible move up the right flank saw Great Britain impossibly stretched, and the mighty Mal Meninga crossed on the left when the ball was worked back across the field. Shades of 1988 again; but we had reckoned without Hanley. As Great Britain built up the pressure once more, their captain added a new trick to his already impressive repertoire by landing an inch-perfect up-and-under on Australian full-back Gary Belcher who, under the heaviest pressure from Daryl Powell and Hanley himself, spilled the ball into the waiting arms of Offiah. The winger had only to fall over the line to score. Schofield added a drop-goal soon after to stretch the lead to 13–6, but the sight of Hanley down injured in some distress must have unnerved his team-mates. As they looked frantically towards him, the giant Kangaroo centre Mark McGaw broke away from several attempted tackles on a brilliant run to score after the last-ditch efforts of Gibson and Hampson had ended in their colliding with each other. At 13–12 it was anyone's game.

Not according to Garry Schofield. With Hanley restored to the fray the stand-off saw his opportunity to break the game with an immaculate chip kick which he regathered himself before haring into the clear. Daryl Powell, as ever, was up in support and the centre timed his pass out to Eastwood with the perfection that allowed the winger a straight sprint to the corner. With two minutes to go, Eastwood clinched an epic victory with a penalty from the touchline; at 19–12, the impossible dream was a reality. Great Britain had taken on Australia at their own game of pressure and professionalism, and added their own blend of skill and innovation to produce the heady brew of triumph.

Great Britain: Hampson (Wigan); Eastwood (Hull), Daryl Powell (Sheffield Eagles), Gibson (Leeds), Offiah (Widnes); Schofield (Leeds), Andy Gregory (Wigan); Harrison (Hull), Jackson (Hull), Dixon (Leeds), Roy Powell (Leeds), Betts (Wigan), Hanley (Wigan)
Substitutes: Ward (St Helens) for Roy Powell after 46 minutes, Fairbank (Bradford Northern) for Harrison after 72 minutes; Edwards (Wigan) and David Hulme (Widnes) not used
Scorers: tries – Eastwood (2), Offiah; goals – Eastwood (3); drop-goal – Schofield

Australia: Belcher; Ettingshausen, McGaw, Meninga, Hancock; Stuart, Langer; Roach, Kerrod Walters, Bella, Sironen, Cartwright, Lindner
Substitutes: Hasler for Cartwright and Lazarus for Bella after 72 minutes, Alexander for Langer after 76 minutes, Shearer for Hancock after 78 minutes
Scorers: tries – Meninga, McGaw; goals – Meninga (2)

Referee: A. Sablayrolles (France)

A huge roar greeted the final whistle, and Bob Ashby, the Rugby Football League chairman's eyes filled as he accepted congratulations from Ken Arthurson, the Australian Rugby League president. He was entitled to feel emotional, and he wasn't the only one in the stadium whose eyes were stinging. So the spectre of Boothferry Park which had haunted us since 1982 had been finally exorcised. It had been a long and painful period of rehabilitation, but now we had defeated Australia in two consecutive matches – the third Test in Sydney and the first Test at Wembley. We could all walk tall again.

Daryl Powell (right) celebrates as Martin Offiah plunges to claim the try after Kangaroo full-back Gary Belcher had spilled Ellery Hanley's precision bomb during the first Test at Wembley in 1990. Langer (No. 7) and Ettingshausen (No. 5) look on.

Bobby Fulton, the Australian coach, was to blame Alain Sabayrolles, the French referee, particularly for the amount of times he had punished Australia for offside offences. What Fulton could not account for, however, was their inability to break down the British defence. His players had been outplayed, and Mal Reilly had outcoached him; that was the harsh, unpalatable truth.

Mal wasn't boastful when I saw him in the dressing-room afterwards – but then I knew he wouldn't be. He was already shaping his strategy for the second British Coal Test at Old Trafford. He and Phil Larder knew from experience that a whole new ball-game lay ahead. What the win had provided, however, was the necessary motivational surge that his players needed. Now they knew they could win the series; they had the ability and they had the belief.

The challenge was to produce another eighty minutes of error-free play. Should Great Britain remain unchanged? Could Mal take the initiative and strengthen the team without damaging morale? In the end, Mal decided to bring in the explosive and fit-again Andy Platt at No. 10 and drop Roy Powell to the substitutes bench. Paul Loughlin, who had also missed the first Test through injury, was included as a substitute. Australia were clearly rattled and made six changes, bringing in Dale Shearer, Laurie Daley, Cliff Lyons, Benny Elias, Glenn Lazarus and Brad Mackay. Many critics felt that this was a better team than the original one.

Australian prop Steve Roach is held by Great Britain second row Paul Dixon as his Lions pack colleagues Denis Betts (No. 11) and Karl Harrison close in, in the second Test at Old Trafford in 1990.

Both coaches had challenging tests. Mal Reilly had to prepare his team knowing that his tactics for the first Test would have been analysed and dissected. The element of surprise had been used and Australia would be an entirely different proposition. Bobby Fulton was now up against it as the humiliation of losing a series to the Poms was a stark possibility. Confidence in the Australian camp had been shaken, and for the first time for years they no longer seemed invincible. This would produce greater commitment from the players, but it would also increase anxiety. A team experiencing stress can be harassed into mistakes as they tend to be more cautious in their play.

The atmosphere at Old Trafford on Saturday 10 November was different to that generated two weeks before at Wembley. Then it had been apprehensive; now it was thirsting for victory, as 46,615 people packed the stadium to watch the drama unfold. Australia ran on to the Old Trafford arena, but Great Britain stalked out in single file, emphasising that they would not allow the atmosphere to distract them – concentration was absolute.

As Great Britain had played the Australian game at Wembley, so now Australia began by playing the British game at a frightening pace, moving the ball rapidly from side to side with Lyons and Stuart, back in his favoured scrum-half berth following a disappointing first Test, driving them on. Great Britain could only hang on grimly, unable to exert the control of Wembley and sucked into the maelstrom of Australia's pattern. Neither Schofield nor Gregory could work the kicking game to advantage, and they suffered by comparison with the lateral scuttles of Lyons and the booming passes of Stuart. Schofield did manage to slip Dixon through near the posts, but the grafting forward failed to ground the ball.

Australian half-back Ricky Stuart breaks away from Karl Harrison (centre) and Andy Platt during the second Test of 1990 at Old Trafford. Stuart gave the pass that Loughlin intercepted to give Great Britain the lead, but it was his last-minute break that gave Mal Meninga the winning try.

After twenty minutes Great Britain were stretched once too often, and Dale Shearer was released down the left to evade Schofield and Hanley in a charge for the line. By half-time Great Britain had clawed 2 points back, but they left the field visibly wearied by the efforts of restraining the Australian attacks. Whatever Mal said at half-time was clearly effective, as Schofield worked the same move with Dixon, who this time crashed through a double tackle for a courageous try. The lead was only temporary, however, as a brilliant bout of interpassing sprang Ettingshausen on the right, and his fifty-metre sprint down the line finished with a perfect cross-kick for Lyons to score a well-deserved try near the posts.

Although the gap between the teams was only 4 points, Great Britain continued to look at breaking point, while their offence, with Hanley diligently marshalled by Mackay, and Offiah off the field with a knee injury, began to look less and less convincing. As Australia launched another threatening attack and Stuart sought the overlap with another long ball, Paul Loughlin, on for Offiah, pounced to snatch the interception and stride away for a sensational try ten minutes from time. Eastwood failed with the conversion, and now it was Australia, the clock and sheer fatigue in mounting opposition to the gallant Great Britain team. With the timekeeper's finger poised to end the game at the next tackle, Ricky Stuart, who minutes earlier had been utterly mortified at his indiscretion for Loughlin's try, took up the play on Australia's 22. Picking out Lee Jackson as one Lion who had worked himself to a standstill, Stuart sold the hooker an outrageous dummy and raced away up the touchline. Without Offiah's pace to run him down, Great Britain's cover scrambled desperately across until Stuart, about to be swamped, lobbed the ball inside to his captain Meninga, who had barged his way upfield in support. The touchdown was the last act of a pulsating drama, and Australia had stolen victory by 14–10.

Great Britain: Hampson (Wigan); Eastwood (Hull), Daryl Powell (Sheffield Eagles), Gibson (Leeds), Offiah (Widnes); Schofield (Leeds), Andy Gregory (Wigan); Harrison (Hull), Jackson (Hull), Platt (Wigan), Dixon (Leeds), Betts (Wigan), Hanley (Wigan)
Substitutes: Loughlin (St Helens) for Offiah after 45 minutes, Ward (St Helens) for Harrison after 51 minutes; Roy Powell (Leeds) and David Hulme (Widnes) not used
Scorers: tries – Dixon, Loughlin; goal – Eastwood

Australia: Belcher; Ettingshausen, Meninga, Laurie Daley, Shearer; Lyons, Stuart; Roach, Elias, Lazarus, Sironen, Lindner, Mackay
Substitutes: Alexander, Hasler, Sargent and Gillespie not used
Scorers: tries – Shearer, Lyons, Meninga; goal – Meninga

Referee: A. Sablayrolles (France)

In the last ten minutes Great Britain had failed to clinch an epic victory, relinquished a share of the spoils and then had to suffer the bitterness of defeat. The despair etched on the faces of the players said it all. They had given everything, and there was nothing left but the agony of defeat when glory had been within their grasp.

When I spoke to Mal Reilly an hour after the match he was totally gutted, the disappointment too much to bear. He knew that fate had conspired against him; although his team had not played as efficiently as he had hoped, to be denied victory when it was so tantalisingly close was hard to come to terms with. I tried to reassure Mal that he had absolutely nothing to reproach himself for, but I did not share my own private thoughts which were that we had perhaps missed our opportunity and that the advantage had now passed to the Australians.

Australia had to fulfil two more club matches before the third British Coal Test and gained wins over Hull and Widnes. The 15–8 victory over Widnes was a competitive match, but it meant that Australia had now completed three consecutive tours of Great Britain without losing to a club side.

For the deciding Test Mal chose the same thirteen that had played in the second Test, but brought in Jonathan Davies and Mike Gregory on the bench. Popular opinion suggested that, as kicking could be crucial, perhaps Davies should start the match. With Offiah the only Great Britain player with genuine pace, and him nursing an injured knee, it was thought that the Welshman might add something to this department, too. Loyalty is a powerful bonding agent, but it perhaps meant that Mal's tactical options were constrained by his commitment to an unchanged line-up.

The stage was set at Elland Road on Saturday 24 November for the final showdown. An emotion-charged atmosphere rose to fever pitch as Great Britain entered the field of play to be met by the singing of *Land of Hope and Glory*, led by a massed choir of 32,000 people. The thirteen players were in no doubt as to the weight of responsibility they shouldered. Yet if Great Britain were determined to win, Australia were equally determined not to lose.

It was in cold, driving rain that Meninga kicked off to establish Australia deep in the Great Britain half, a position they were to retain for much of the match. This time it was the old Australia, putting on an error-free performance of ruthless efficiency, exerting maximum pressure wherever they sensed a weakness. This was best illustrated in the ninth minute when, with Gibson receiving treatment for a head injury and his replacement Davies not yet on the field, Stuart realised that Great Britain's left flank was undermanned and exposed and spun a huge cut-out ball to Ettingshausen, who charged into the corner.

Great Britain launched a brave recovery, Betts breaking away from Andy Gregory's pass, but the covering Australians never allowed him to link with the supporting Schofield and he was submerged in a three-man tackle. Then Hampson charged down a speculative kick on his own 22 and put Davies away, but the substitute had not travelled twenty metres before he was cut down by an exemplary cover tackle from Stuart. At half-time the score was only 4–0 to Australia, but the gulf between the sides was much wider than that.

Mal had a difficult decision at the interval, whether to carry on with the starting thirteen in the hope that they would recover the Wembley spirit, or to introduce David Hulme for the ineffectual Andy Gregory and Roy Powell and Mike Gregory for Harrison and Dixon in the hope that the substitutes might redirect the play. In the end he opted for the former, and Great Britain mounted a stirring comeback in the second half, but still never looked like scoring. Australia's dominance was reflected in one shuddering tackle by Sironen on Hanley in which the Great Britain captain was stopped dead in his tracks and bounced to the ground, in a dramatic, 'they shall not pass' scenario. Then Lyons created a superb try for Meninga and, finally, Daley broke from acting half-back in his own 22 and, although

Paul Dixon, supported by Leeds club-mate Garry Schofield, drives the ball forward into the tackle of Australia's Bob Lindner in the second Test in 1990. Dixon and Lindner were perhaps their respective teams' most consistent forwards throughout the series.

Davies floored him with a brilliant cover tackle fifty metres downfield, the man-of-the-match, Elias, playing through the pain of broken ribs, dived under a three-man tackle to score in the corner. At 14–0 it was all over, although fears that the floodgates would open in the closing stages proved groundless as Australia's attempts to increase the score foundered on the stubborn defence of a still proud and courageous Great Britain team. In the end, Mal's men were defeated by a magnificent team, and there was no disgrace in that.

Great Britain: Hampson (Wigan); Eastwood (Hull), Daryl Powell (Sheffield Eagles), Gibson (Leeds), Offiah (Widnes); Schofield (Leeds), Andy Gregory (Wigan); Harrison (Hull), Jackson (Hull), Platt (Wigan), Dixon (Leeds), Betts (Wigan), Hanley (Wigan)
Substitutes: Davies (Widnes) for Gibson after 9 minutes, Mike Gregory (Warrington) for Dixon after 55 minutes, Roy Powell (Leeds) for Harrison after 73 minutes; David Hulme (Widnes) not used

Australia: Belcher; Ettingshausen, Meninga, Laurie Daley, Shearer; Lyons, Stuart; Roach, Elias, Lazarus, Sironen, Lindner, Mackay
Substitutes: Alexander for Shearer after 76 minutes, Hasler for Mackay after 76 minutes, Sargent for Lazarus after 76 minutes, Gillespie for Sironen after 76 minutes
Scorers: tries – Ettingshausen, Meninga, Elias; goal – Meninga

Referee: A. Sablayrolles (France)

10

The Way Ahead

In documenting Great Britain's revival at international level since 1985 I had hoped for a happy ending – a Test series victory over Australia after twenty barren years. Mal Reilly's team had been close to achieving it but in the end had to settle for taking part in the most competitive series since Great Britain last won in 1970. Nevertheless, British Rugby League convincingly demonstrated that, in five years, it had dragged itself from obscurity to be able to compete against the world champions. The whole game had faced up to the challenge and tackled the task of raising standards at every level. It was no overnight miracle – but then no one ever expected it was going to be easy to reverse the years of complacency and neglect that were exposed at Boothferry Park in 1982.

Although British Rugby League has indeed closed the gap, the 1990 Test series still suggested that the product of the Sydney League is superior to that of the British League. At international level Great Britain are as experienced and sophisticated in preparing international teams as Australia, and Mal Reilly and Phil Larder can stand comparison with the best. But we will not be able to gain real supremacy over Australia until standards in our domestic competition match those in Sydney.

The major challenge facing our game in the immediate future is to focus on improving player development and production. The critical years are 9 to 17, when boys develop the fundamental skills of Rugby League. Unless there is a structure that provides quality coaching and first-class graded competitions for that age-group we will not be able to produce sufficient skilled players. There are, of course, enormous logistical, organisational and resource implications, but it is an issue that has to be addressed as a matter of priority. The more youngsters taking part and playing Rugby League, the more likely we are to produce sufficient players with the skills and attitude to match their Australian counterparts.

Tom O'Donovan, the BARLA National Development Officer, and his expanding team of regional development officers are working incredibly hard to close the gap, as are the products of Phil Larder's National Coaching Scheme. The challenge of producing quality players, however, cannot be tackled piecemeal. A strong network of schools teams, youth teams and student teams will not only make Rugby League stronger and produce quality players at each level, but will also ensure the game's future in the face of competition from rival sports.

To survive and prosper, we have to recognise that we are engaged in an intense, cut-throat battle with all the other spectator sports. Each in turn is affected by the vagaries of social trends, market forces, inflation, the economy and media interest. Each is competing for a share of the sports entertainment market, as the total amount spent on sport is a variable percentage of the family entertainment budget. Should Rugby League begin to lose its appeal, harsh economic reality would see the game slide into obscurity.

In maintaining our present position, one fundamental question has to be addressed. Do we settle for remaining a professional sport played more or less exclusively in the north of England – to be more specific, by thirty-six clubs, the majority of which straddle the M62 motorway – or do we persist in the dream of establishing professional clubs in leading cities throughout the length and breadth of England?

The reality is that the majority of existing clubs are not financially viable and cannot survive through the proceeds collected at the turnstiles, but rely on cash generated by professional fund-raisers, sponsorship, transfer fees, and substantial financial backing from club chairmen and directors. The product is excellent, but attendances as a whole are not increasing at a substantial rate. Test matches and cup finals are the game's showpieces and are attracting increased patronage, but the game's thrusting and dynamic image is in the main generated by a small proportion of first-division clubs, along with the national team.

Hull hooker Lee Jackson gets the ball away from acting half-back. Jackson overcame the rival claims of Martin Dermott and Phil McKenzie for the No. 9 jersey for the Kangaroo series, and gave three most impressive displays.

Economists could calculate fairly accurately the amount of finance and number of spectators generated by the existing club set-up and conclude that a reduction in the number of professional clubs would not adversely affect either. However, teams going out of business because of debt cause incalculable damage to the image of the sport and would be counter-productive. The gradual erosion of the number of teams in the RFL would sound the alarm bells for the whole game. It would be one thing to restructure the game as part of an agreed policy; it would be a different thing entirely, to arrive at a slimmed-down professional league by default.

The pressing need for restructuring the old two divisions into three has been top of the agenda for several years. It was never pursued with any great enthusiasm, however, as not all clubs welcomed it, but it suddenly gained impetus in 1991 with the production of a formula by Gary Hetherington of Sheffield. This imaginative format proposed a first division of fourteen clubs, a second division of eight and a third division of fourteen. Despite its unevenness, dissatisfaction with the current situation produced an unexpected ground swell of opinion in favour of adopting it.

A special general meeting called on 6 March, however, broke up in acrimony as the motion was defeated by two votes. There were veiled threats of breakaway, and accusations of sabotage were levelled at several clubs labelled 'unprogressive'. In the end common sense prevailed and the Hetherington plan was resubmitted by the board of directors to be considered at a special general meeting on 17 April. Despite a spirited attempt by Castleford to gain support for three equal divisions of twelve, the new league structure based on the Hetherington plan was adopted for 1991–92. It was a close-run thing, and one vote tipped the balance.

There is still a pressing need for an overall reduction in the number of games played by top players in order to minimise wear and tear and possibly to improve the quality of play. Top players, however, are still pursuing lucrative contracts in Australia which negates the wear and tear argument. A reduction in games will come about eventually, I believe, and I certainly welcome the advent of three divisions. Nevertheless, the new format will be a stern test for the less successful clubs who may fear that natural wastage will lead to the dissolution of the third division. In this regard, there is always one overriding factor, and that is an incredible will to survive which defies logic. The people responsible for running Rugby League clubs have a passion and optimism which rises above depressing bank overdrafts, and somehow they continue to find a way.

I now believe that for the good of the game the Rugby Football League and the British Amateur Rugby League Association should merge. Although BARLA was given a mandate by the RFL in 1973 to assume total responsibility for the amateur game, I do not believe that continued separation benefits either body. A new constitution embracing the professional game, BARLA, schools and colleges could be negotiated that guarantees certain rights to each organisation. If East and West Germany can merge after forty-five years I am sure that Rugby League can and should exist under one umbrella.

A development policy would channel all existing resources and energies into a co-ordinated approach. The professional game is the flagship and it needs to be strong to ensure continued sponsorship and public and media interest. The professional game, however, is inextricably linked to the amateurs, and it needs a strong and efficient supporting network of amateur clubs which in turn rely on a supply of youngsters from the schools. If we need the schools to provide a supply of youngsters keen to play Rugby League then that question has to be tackled by the game as a whole. Amateur clubs more and more are developing their own junior teams, but they desperately need pitches, equipment, facilities, coaches and adult helpers.

Garry Schofield (second right) completed his transformation from try-scoring centre to world-class stand-off with a masterly display against Australia at Wembley in 1990, controlling the match with his kicking and prompting.

The professional game cannot leave all this to chance by simply channelling funds to schools, BARLA, the National Coaching Scheme and a growing number of development officers. This leads to a fragmented approach as, although each organisation complements the others, they all have considerable autonomy. I believe that one governing body with the single aim of promoting Rugby League should be our goal. Now is the time for one bold step and 1995, the centenary of the breakaway from Rugby Union and the formation of the Rugby Football League, could be the target date.

Although the game is committed to expansion, in reality it has no policy on this issue. Expansion, when it has taken place, has occurred by chance as the result of a small group of entrepreneurs and enthusiasts getting together and seeking support from the governing body. That is not a policy of expansion and is reactive, not pro-active. Central initiatives in the name of expansion have amounted to the playing of one-off matches under the banner of promotion. In 1990 the Charity Shield match between Wigan and Widnes at Swansea achieved absolutely nothing as there was no follow-up to it in terms of coaching courses, establishing new amateur teams or, indeed, using the match to launch a professional team in South Wales.

An expansion policy would target key cities, decide on a timescale, allocate funding and then seek to launch by putting together a promotional package. This would involve identifying key businessmen in the expansion area who have access to finance and are prepared to join a consortium. The presentation campaign would have to include a detailed portfolio of all that would be required to establish a professional club – players, finance, facilities, sponsorship, coaching – and would make clear the level of backing, advice and finance available from the governing body. There would need to be publicity, exhibition matches – in short, a planned, co-ordinated campaign.

What I have described is the minimum that would have to happen for Rugby League to be played successfully in Leicester, Birmingham, Bath, Bristol or Exeter. It is unlikely to happen because the Rugby Football League has not got the financial resources or manpower to make it happen, and the RFL's member clubs are not interested in diverting precious central resources to speculative ventures when they themselves need every available penny. In fact their generosity in allowing the current level of financial support for development is commendable when they could use it themselves. Already each member club has contributed £25,000 to the central development budget, and yet the overall amount is well short of what is needed to promote Rugby League in the north of England, let alone subsidise professional clubs elsewhere. Indeed, it is arguable that professional clubs should demand a greater share of increased central revenue, and that their welfare should be the top priority.

Fulham, despite a meteoric start, hang on by the skin of their teeth in the metropolis. In terms of professional sport it is an irrelevance with an average crowd of under 1,000. If Fulham cannot establish themselves after a decade, then the future for expansion is bleak. There may be interested TV audiences in the south of England, but I do not believe that the same people would necessarily watch live Rugby League even if there was a team within travelling distance. Even if resources to establish the professional game in other areas were forthcoming, there is no guarantee of a successful transplant.

Where expansion is taking place, with varied success, is in the amateur ranks where BARLA have worked hard to support the birth of new teams in London, the South-West, Wales and the Midlands. The challenge for an amateur team to recruit players, find a ground, purchase equipment, and raise funds just to survive, however, is daunting and every year teams succumb to the strain and collapse. A strong network of amateur teams in a development area might ultimately lead to a professional team there, but time alone will determine that eventuality.

Where does that leave us? I believe our first duty is to promote and consolidate Rugby League within the existing league structure, because our ultimate responsibility is to ensure survival within the competitive world of sport. There is every indication that we are equipped to succeed providing we focus on the quality of our product on the field of play and continue to improve facilities for spectators. We may be isolated in the north of England but we have a relatively high profile nationwide, and that attracts media coverage and potential sponsors.

Throughout its history the game has always had the capacity and courage to adapt to changing conditions. The present six-tackle game gives scope for all the best features of rugby – spectacular running, movement of the ball and crushing tackles. Despite the current emphasis on defence there are more points being scored than in the 1970s when the six-tackle game was in its embryonic stage. The value of effective kicking to relieve pressure, gain ground and break up the defensive line encourages movement and ensures a rapid change-over of possession which maintains and stimulates spectator interest.

To cope with the explosive nature of the modern game overall fitness levels have risen dramatically. Teams now train three times a week, and players are also expected to put in additional work in their own time. Because the financial rewards for success have increased, the game is not regarded as a diversion that brings in a little extra money for the

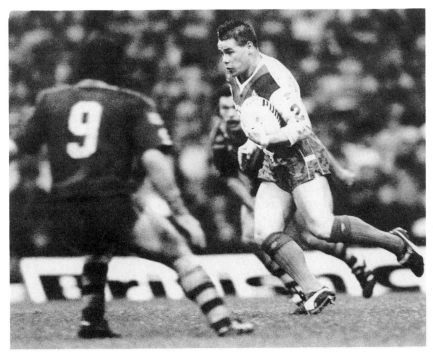

Paul Eastwood was Great Britain's hero at Wembley in 1990, scoring two tries to exorcise his own personal ghost of Jonathan Davies, his rival for the wing position. Yet his goal-kicking in the next two Tests may well have cost Great Britain the series.

very successful; professional Rugby League is a full-time occupation which sustains an attractive lifestyle for an increasing number of players.

I do not believe that players of today are more skilful than players of other decades. A good player is a good player, and that is an eternal truth in the world of sport. But the intensity of the fight for survival, let alone success, in the first division in the 1990s has had a dramatic effect overall. Any player who cannot match the demands of the first division is soon discarded as clubs and coaches constantly pursue success. Most players today are more tactically aware than the majority of players of my era. The six-tackle game has a recognisable format, and statistics and video analysis reinforce the work of the coach. Teams have game plans, they employ specific defence ploys, they are motivated to meet personal goals – in short, the world of contemporary British Rugby League is a product of the whole revolutionary process which had as its role model the intense Sydney League.

In an effort to raise playing standards in the 1980s there was the wholesale recruitment of top Australian and New Zealand players. A quota restriction of three per club has since brought the situation under control, because of its potential long-term damage to the home-grown market. Now we have an interesting trend developing in the coaching world as clubs have sought to recruit overseas coaches following the success of Graham Lowe at Wigan.

What disturbs me about this is that short-sighted club directors and blinkered club coaches failed to respond in a positive way to the efforts of the coaching committee and the National Coaching Scheme to improve the education of coaches. Many were hostile to the scheme and its aims when their support was absolutely vital to give it credibility. The price of that neglect is now being paid as clubs have recruited overseas coaches in the mistaken belief that they must be superior to our own; some of the British coaches deposed by this invasion are the ones who missed the opportunity to support Phil Larder's National Coaching Scheme. The appointment of coaches from abroad who are prepared to attend courses, meetings, conferences and gain qualifications has raised the profile of coaching, but British coaches should have responded to the challenge earlier.

The quality of coaching staff is the critical factor in raising the overall level of playing standards, and the more professional coaches become, the more our game will benefit. They have the greatest influence on the quality of play, and a proper training and recruitment system underpins everything.

My view is that throughout the three divisions now we have coaches as dedicated and committed as their overseas contemporaries. Each coach is different, of course, and each has unique qualities, but men such as Mal Reilly, Peter Fox, Doug Laughton, Alex Murphy, Roger Millward and Allan Agar represent all that is special about Rugby League. Younger men such as David Ward, Dave Topliss, David Hobbs and Gary Hetherington represent the newer breed of coach. Fortunately many of the current crop of top players are already gaining qualifications to fit them for future coaching positions.

No longer can clubs rely on one coach to do everything. They must realise that a team of managers, coaches, fitness experts and medical staff – each man with skills and knowledge in specific areas – is required if success is to be achieved. Some excellent coaches are not suited to the stresses of being a manager, while excellent managers, such as Peter Fox of Featherstone and Doug Laughton of Leeds, are quite happy to delegate certain aspects of team preparation to assistants. The days of one man attempting everything should be a thing of the past.

If, in its effort to present itself as a spectacle full of excitement and entertainment, the game continues to adapt and refine itself, the three changes most likely to be considered in the future are scrummaging, the number of players in the team and player equipment. Already there is a lobby to abandon scrums because of their untidy appearance and blatant disregard for rules. I would regret the demise of scrums because they break up the general pattern of play and provide room for back play. Already scrums have reduced in number in my time from an average of fifty per match to as few as eighteen, while earlier in the game's history scrums exceeded eighty. My crystal ball, therefore, tells me that scrums will disappear altogether.

I also believe that the number of players in the team could be reduced to eleven with four to six substitutes. The game's legislators, in pursuit of fast-flowing, high-scoring entertainment, could be tempted to consider this, in the same way that the number of players was reduced from fifteen to thirteen earlier in the century. It is also possible that the legislators could consider moving to a March–September season, with Wednesday evenings becoming 'League night'. This is unlikely to be considered for some time, but I would not rule out its potential if the competition for spectators hotted up or social habits at weekends changed.

As playing kit continues to become more colourful, I also predict that safety equipment such as shoulder pads, thigh pads and helmets will become an increasing feature of the game. When I played, no one wore gum shields; now every player regards them as essential. One of the appeals of American Football is the players' spaceman appearance, which accentuates their physical presence and 'superman' status. Will our game take on board such developments, not only for safety reasons but as part of its marketing strategy?

Marketing will play a key role in ensuring our share of the sports-entertainment market as we move through the 1990s. At present the emphasis is on the merchandising of clothing and videos along with the new '13' logo. Marketing the game of Rugby League, however, is not the same as merchandising, and at present no marketing budget or strategy exists, either in the Rugby Football League or in the individual clubs. In the modern world of hype and promotion this needs to be rectified so that the game of Rugby League is promoted to capture the imagination of the public and attract new supporters and sponsors, in the way that the Australian Rugby League hired the incredible Tina Turner to produce the famous video *Simply the Best*.

Marketing is expensive because TV advertising slots are costly. Nevertheless, we have the marketable image of a visually exciting collision sport that still sustains sporting values, is not divorced from its public, appeals to the family and has integrity. These are the qualities and values that need to be promoted through TV, videos, records, posters, books, magazines, publicity campaigns, exhibitions and clothing. At present we have hardly dipped our toe into the water; soon we will have to take the plunge.

Daryl Powell, the first player from the Sheffield Eagles club to be capped by Great Britain, had a splendid run in Tests in 1990, and was involved in all three Great Britain tries in the momentous win over Australia at Wembley.

In attracting spectators we have to hold on to the ones we have got, and then seek ways of enticing new people to watch Rugby League. That means not only maintaining the quality of the product on the pitch, but also improving our stadia which, in the main, still lag behind in standards of cleanliness and comfort. The Taylor Report has led to massive improvements in ground safety, and clubs have responded well to legislation. The overall cost throughout the game has exceeded £3 million, and I suppose spectators are entitled to say 'not before time'. Most of our stadia were built over fifty years ago, and to modernise a stadium piecemeal is difficult and expensive, but the Rugby Football League is working towards its own minimum standards guidelines with great determination.

I see ground-sharing as inevitable in the future. One ideal development would be for local authorities to build central facilities, such as the Sheffield project, which caters for various sports. Rugby League clubs would then be relieved of the immense burden of having to maintain stadia, with all the expense involved for one game a week. The local authority would maintain the facility and clubs would be responsible for the hire charge. Not every club would want that arrangement, but for many clubs it would ensure survival.

We owe all this to spectators who in the past have been taken for granted. The game now attracts a good cross-section of the age range, which is reassuring as at one time we seemed to have an ageing group of spectators. Rugby League supporters are marvellous people, friendly and passionate about the game. They enjoy the homeliness of our grounds and the camaraderie. They will support the game through thick and thin, but we need more of them. I see these coming from soccer and Rugby Union, as well as from the uncommitted. The way to attract them is to project our game, not as superior to soccer and Rugby Union, but as an alternative. We need to persuade sports fans to watch our game on Sundays because they will enjoy it and find it interesting. Most people who enjoy sport are capable of sustaining interest in more than one.

Televised matches are now part of a promotional strategy and are responsible for a substantial part of the game's central income – it is now approaching £3 million, which is used to recompense clubs for loss of revenue and also diverted to central funds for development and loans. Interest from TV companies has accelerated, and the BBC no longer have the monopoly. There is an underlying worry, however, that the game could suffer from over-exposure, and there have been examples of that with other sports. Boxing was practically killed off as a popular spectator sport in America as audiences stayed at home to watch in their living rooms. The situation will need careful monitoring to analyse cause and effect if crowd figures fall.

TV is here to stay, however, and we need exposure. We have an excellent TV image, and the game comes across as first-class viewing. TV companies are also packaging the game in a more interesting way so that viewers become better informed. We have a tiger by the tail; we need to be vigilant and hang on.

The challenge on all fronts is enormous, but we have the capacity to succeed. That is why a comprehensive and overall development policy that embraces every facet of the game has to be produced as a matter of urgency if we are to stay in the race. Although progress is being made on most fronts, a co-ordinated strategy is essential if it is to have any coherence. It will certainly be more complex than anything attempted before. It will involve consultations with influential people in every sector of the game because, unless people feel part of a development policy, it is unlikely to happen. The workload will be tremendous: submissions from informed representatives, both written and verbal, will need to be collected and collated; there will be a need for different working groups to be set up to examine and research all aspects of Rugby League. The expertise already exists within the game but is waiting to be tapped and co-ordinated.

Unless we produce such a major policy document, we may fail to realise our full potential and dissipate our energy thrashing about and arguing over day-to-day crises. We need a vision, and 1995 is the ideal date to launch that vision. Rugby League is our legacy; we hold it in trust with an obligation to pass it on to the next generation in good shape. All of us have a stake in promoting the game we love, and we cannot abdicate that responsibility. We have to guard against complacency and inertia if the vision of the future is to be achieved.

I am as excited by the game now as when I played my first game for Millom a lifetime ago. In that time the game has changed, but the very essence of Rugby League – its integrity – remains intact. Here's to the next 100 years!